My Friend

FOOTY

My Friend

FOOTY

A Memoir of Paul Foot
by Richard Ingrams

*Caroline
with love
Richard
Oct 05*

PRIVATE EYE

Published in Great Britain
by Private Eye Productions Ltd,
6 Carlisle Street, London W1D 3BN

© 2005 Pressdram Ltd
ISBN 1 901784 42 8
Designed by Bridget Tisdall
Printed in England by
Clays Ltd, St Ives plc

Introduction

On 12 July 2004, at what had become our regular fortnightly lunch date in Soho, I discovered that Paul Foot and I were both going to be on holiday in southern Ireland at the same time the following week. We arranged to meet up and swapped telephone numbers, so when the phone rang in Ireland that Sunday night I was half expecting it to be Paul. Instead it was my son Fred with the devastating news that Paul had collapsed and died at Stansted airport, just as he was about to board the plane for Ireland.

His funeral, which took place at Golders Green on 27 July, was an astonishing affair. An estimated 2,000 people followed the hearse the half a mile or so up the main road from the tube station to the crematorium.

There were banners from trade unions and the Socialist Workers Party; at the head of the procession were Clare, his partner for over 15 years, and their daughter Kate, his ex-wives Monica and Rose, his three sons John, Matt and Tom, his uncle Michael, and many other relatives and friends from the world of journalism.

Some well-known faces were in the throng, including Bruce Kent, Tony Benn and George Galloway; others would only have been recognised by a few, among them the people he had campaigned for over the years – Ann Whelan, the mother of one of the Bridgewater Three Michael Hickey, and Colin Wallace the former army intelligence officer. There were far too many people to fit inside the chapel, and the overflow stood outside in the sunshine and listened to a relay of the speeches.

The service, if you could call it that, had no religious content, in accordance with Paul's atheism. It always annoys me when this happens, because although the wishes of the deceased should be respected, there will always be quite a lot of people at a funeral with religious beliefs who feel a void. When my turn came to speak I mentioned the fact, to laughter, that Paul had been rather annoyed on being told that, when he was close to death in hospital a few years previously, some of us had been praying for him – and even more annoyed that when he made what seemed like a miraculous recovery, those same people claimed that their prayers had helped to bring it about. "There is nothing to stop us now," I ended, "from praying that our beloved Footy may rest in peace." Afterwards I was relieved to be thanked by two Catholics – George Galloway and the former Monsignor Bruce Kent.

From the speeches and the tributes at Golders Green, two distinct Footies emerged. One was the Socialist Worker celebrated by his fellow members Jim Nichol and Lindsey German, the comrade who, with his speeches and articles, had drawn the bulk of the crowd which flocked to the crematorium. The other emerged in the more personal tributes from his sons, who stressed his love of things like French cricket but, more importantly, his love of jokes and second-hand books – jokes especially.

A small group of people at the funeral, myself included, felt rather uncomfortable with the political

Footy. When the service ended with the singing of the Internationale, Anthony Sampson wrote later that "we could not quite bring ourselves to raise our clenched fists as the congregation sang 'Arise ye starvelings from your slumbers'". It was not necessarily that we felt at odds with the sentiment, but this strident chorus and the clenched fists didn't quite fit with the friend I had known.

A few months after the funeral I edited a 12-page supplement in Private Eye as a tribute to Paul, and it occurred to me that I could write at greater length about our collaborations over the years in recognition of the personal debt I owed him.

As reactions to the funeral showed, Paul lived a double life and his friends tended to be in one camp or the other. Fellow Marxists will insist that his political beliefs inspired all his journalism, but that is only partly true. Looking back at his longest and best-known campaigns, I find that he undertook them more for the sake of helping individuals battling for justice, rather than from any urge to discredit "the system".

This short memoir makes no attempt to describe or explain his political activities, and for that reason it may disappoint the comrades. Nor does it purport to be a full-scale biography of the type that would uncover his rather complex private life. Someone else may one day do the job thoroughly. What follows is my own memoir of my best friend. But because my memory is so patchy I have been helped by a number of others, especially Tariq Ali, Geoffrey Bindman, Gus Macdonald, Jean McCrindle, Peter Jay, Monica Foot, Rose Foot, Harry Thompson, Michael Charlesworth, Ian Hislop, Hilary Lowinger and all the staff at Private Eye. My special thanks to Jeremy Lewis for his expert editorial skills.

When I arrived at University College Oxford in the autumn of 1958 almost the first person I saw was my old schoolfellow from Shrewsbury, Paul Foot. He remembered our meeting at dinner in Hall that evening. I remembered him standing on the steps of the college. Whoever was right, the fact is that we fell on one another.

Coming up to Oxford, knowing no one, was alarming enough. But to those of us in the days of National Service, who had been away from academic work for two or three years, it was especially daunting. Most of those sitting in Hall that night had come straight from school. We felt older and, if not wiser, then different. I certainly did not feel particularly like going back to Latin proses and Greek texts. As it turned out we were both lucky to have ended up at Univ, where the dons took a rather more lenient view of National Service undergraduates than they did at some other colleges. There was a predominance of public school rugger-playing types ('bloodies'), but the atmosphere was one of tolerance especially where work was concerned.

After dinner that first evening, we both adjourned to Paul's rooms, conveniently situated in the top right-hand corner of the front quad above the JCR. I discovered that he was reading Law, that his hero was Bernard Shaw and that he was sharing rooms with a fellow law student Tim Pugh – a very tolerant, long-suffering character who years later committed suicide, though how or why I have never discovered. Paul showed me a telegram he had received from his father, Sir Hugh Foot, recently appointed Governor of Cyprus – "Get a First and be President of the Union". (He achieved the second but not the first.)

It was and still is easy to sink without trace at Oxford, or any large university for that matter. I was very conscious of the way my elder brother

P.J., who had been a 'figure' at Shrewsbury – actor, musician, athlete, winner of prizes, editor of the school magazine – had disappointed his friends by failing to follow it up at Oxford. The reason, I imagine, was that the competition seemed daunting after being a big fish in a small pond. Oxford seemed like a very big pond, teeming with fish.

I might have gone the same way if it had not been for Paul. I doubt if I would have dared, in our first term, to audition for the OUDS production of Coriolanus if I had had to go along on my own. As it was, we went together, having rehearsed a scene from a one-act play by John Mortimer about prep-school masters called "What Shall We Tell Caroline?".

By Oxford standards the production was to be quite a grand affair with a professional actress, Susan Engel, playing Volumnia, a professional designer (Sean Kenny) and a professional producer Anthony Page from the Royal Court. Page, an intense left-wing figure who conducted rehearsals in a crouching position, looked rather baffled when Paul and I did our Mortimer scene in front and him and OUDS president Patrick Garland (Coriolanus), but we both got small parts, he as a senator and I as a soldier. I can't now find Paul's name in the programme, so he must have been refused permission by his tutor to take part and performed incognito. Later he developed a fascination with Coriolanus. We both went to Stratford in 1959 to see Olivier play the role and Paul subsequently saw just about every production of the play, having convinced himself that it proved that Shakespeare had been a Marxist in all but name.

Accounts of the origins of Private Eye all suggest a group of close friends at Shrewsbury working on the school magazine. But it wasn't really like that. Shrewsbury in the early Fifties was a very old-fashioned school. It was dominated by the teaching of the Classics and boys who studied other subjects were left feeling inferior. Paul and I sat together in the Classical Sixth for a year and I introduced him to the school magazine. He said later that he had hero-worshipped me at school and I was probably aware of this and teased him as a result. What I liked was his enthusiasm. He went to see Olivier's Richard III film nineteen times and could recite most of it by heart. But I would not say that we were friends at school.

In common with most public schools, Shrewsbury was divided up into 'houses', little schools within a school each with its housemaster and house prefects. Friendships with boys in other houses were discouraged, as were friendships with boys in a different age group. Although he was only three months younger, Paul was in a junior year to me. He was also in a different house, School House, whose housemaster was Anthony Chenevix-Trench, an old boy of the school, a brilliant classical scholar and a wartime prisoner of the Japanese.

Trench was a boyish figure with great charm and a natural rapport with schoolboys. I remember him as an inspiring classics teacher, hero-worshipped by my elder brother. It was later said in mitigation by his supporters that his passion for beating small boys was somehow a consequence of his ill-treatment by the Japanese. However, the novelist Francis King, who was a schoolboy contemporary of his at Shrewsbury, points out in his memoirs that even at an early stage in his career Trench had been a keen beater. If he had been a crude sadist of the Dr Squeers variety, he might have done less harm. But Trench was a more sophisticated abuser.

Paul, who became one of his victims, recalled that his technique, at least at Shrewsbury, was to pick on young boys who were doing classics and offer them help with their work. "He announced that if there were fewer than three mistakes in the work, I would get a piece of chocolate, if more than three

Chenevix-Trench as Headmaster of Eton

mistakes, a beating... three mistakes could easily be found. A beating was certain, but then to my relief the prospect of the cane diminished. Trench explained that I had a 'choice' – the cane with trousers on, or the strap with trousers off. There was no choice really though Trench enormously enjoyed watching me make it."

He could not have imagined that the nervous little boy who had caught his eye would one day play a major role in demolishing his reputation. Many years later in 1969 when Paul was working at Private Eye we were visited by Hume Shawcross, son of the distinguished lawyer and Nuremberg prosecutor Hartley Shawcross, whom Trench had just expelled from Eton where he was now headmaster, along with Caspar Fleming, son of the James Bond creator Ian. The resulting 'Footnote' story titled "Jolly Beating Weather" described recent goings on at Eton and the headmaster's continuing use of the cane, showing that his habits had not changed since the Shrewsbury days.

"Rumours that Mr Trench will be retiring," Paul wrote, "were being strenuously denied in official circles this Easter" (Eye 191). Three months later Eton parents were informed that the headmaster was to leave at the end of the summer term.

The surprising thing about Trench's career was that even after his downfall at Eton and the revelations in the Eye, he went on to be given another Headmastership – at Tony Blair's old school, Fettes. Reports suggested that he had failed to mend his ways and that his drinking (which was mentioned at Eton as an additional problem) had become heavier. He died aged only 60 in 1979.

Some years later, an adulatory biography by Mark Law dismissed Paul's attack on his old housemaster as a symptom of his left-wing politics, a useful means of discrediting the public school system and for getting his own back on his own school. In fact, as Paul himself noted when reviewing the biography for the London Review of Books, he had enjoyed his time at Shrewsbury "especially in my last year when Trench was replaced at School House by Michael Charlesworth, a kind and courteous man quite the opposite of his predecessor". Charlesworth made Paul Head of House and he introduced a liberal regime with no beatings. Our mutual friend, the historian Piers Brendon, was also in School House and remembered Paul reading P.G. Wodehouse to the boys in his dormitory and reducing them all to hysterics after lights out.

The most lasting thing we both gained from Shrewsbury was the teaching of Frank McEachran always known as Kek and still remembered with affection by generations of Salopians lucky enough to be taught by him.

A bald, rather gnomelike figure with a bow tie and an accent that was hard to pin down, Kek gave the impression of being somehow detached from the rest of the staff, many of whom were old boys of the school. Little was known about his background except that he had taught at Gresham's School, Holt, and was rumoured to be a friend of W.H. Auden. Having already sat in his classroom for a year, it was fun to see boys like Paul begin by mocking his methods and then slowly be converted. He had a chair out in front of the class and boys were made in turn to come out. "Stand on the chair, boy," Kek would say, and some unfortunate would have to get up and recite some lines of Yeats or T.S. Eliot. These were his 'spells', little extracts of prose or poetry in many different languages – Kek was a multilinguist – chosen to impress on us the sound rather than the meaning of great literature. Sometimes these would be recited in unison by the whole class.

Any of those who sat in Kek's class, as Paul and I did, had a lasting bond in that we had in our heads these little spells and could recite them to one another for the rest of our lives. Paul would have said that a great many people influenced him in his early years – his uncle Michael, Colwyn Williamson, T. Cliff – but my feeling is that Kek's influence was greater and more lasting.

Not that there was anything specifically political about his teaching. He was, we discovered later, a follower of the Liberal economist Henry George, but I don't remember Kek ever referring to him. On the other hand, many of the spells – especially those by Auden or Eliot – struck a subversive note, as did Ezra Pound's verdict on the First World War:

> *There died a myriad*
> *And of the best among them*
> *For an old bitch gone in the teeth*
> *And a botched civilisation*

Today, when schools think nothing of putting on "Oh What a Lovely War" as the school play, it is quite hard to envisage the impact of lines like that on boys like Paul and me, brought up on Shakespeare and Milton and expected to be able to translate A.E. Housman into Latin or Greek; the kind of exercise that Chenevix Trench could do brilliantly.

What with Kek, the plays, the concert choir and the cricket, Paul loved his schooldays probably more than I did. After he left he wrote to Michael Charlesworth, "That last week I was taciturn because, simply, I could not bear to go and could not drive myself to forced heartiness". He would not have liked to be reminded of such romantic thoughts, least of all a subsequent letter to Charlesworth which included this, on his time at Shrewsbury, "I remember far more good than evil. Journalist yes. Socialist yes. But always an upholder

John Davis posing as a Don lecturing to his only student (Paul)

of the Public Schools. We may find each other in that last ditch".

Even when he was at Oxford Paul was still keeping in touch with his old housemaster. "This is my idea of Paradise on Earth," he wrote to Charlesworth. "It is extraordinary how many opportunities just sit there to be taken. I seem to spend most of my time in amazement at the joy of the place." This could just as well have been me or any of our contemporaries, especially those of us who had done two years' National Service. I remember hearing Ken Loach, who was President of the OUDS and later, like Paul, a convert to Trotskyism, speaking in almost the same terms. It was the freedom that was the most obvious attraction – freedom to come and go as you pleased, meet in pubs, to choose what lectures to go to, to talk late into the night over endless cups of Nescafe.

And then there were girls, particularly welcome to both Paul and me after our all-male school and army life. I have since read accounts of our Oxford scene as if there were orgies in progress almost daily and as if I myself was a noted sex fiend. But this does not accord with my memories. If, as the poet Larkin maintained, sex began in 1963, we were just a bit too early for it. Both Paul and I, in any case, had steady girlfriends and like all first-time lovers were convinced that we were experiencing something uniquely beautiful. Our Oxford girls were more like groupies who came round to Paul's room for tea and cake and to help, when they were allowed to, in the magazine work.

The journalistic scene at Oxford in those days was not exactly welcoming to people like Paul and myself. The famous magazine Isis had been taken over by the so-called New Left, devotees of CND and readers of Raymond Williams and Richard Hoggart. Their leader was the red-headed miner's son Denis Potter, later to become famous as a television playwright. (Paul invited him to address the Liberal Club of which at the time he was President and he excited us all by announcing that whenever he saw a Rolls Royce he spat at it.) No one would have minded the politics of Potter and his confreres. What Paul objected to, as he would do throughout his life, was the unwillingness of journalists on the left to write clearly or to entertain.

An exception to the generally nondescript character of Oxford journalism was a little pocket-sized magazine called Parson's Pleasure which had been started at Christ Church by Adrian Berry, son of Michael (later Lord Hartwell). Berry was a charming and very wild young man who filled his magazine with esoteric gossip quite unintelligible to people outside the wealthy public school set at Christ Church. (I remember a joke item saying that in future any undergraduate found in the college not wearing Cavalry Twill trousers would be penalised. It was a case, Berry said, of "Harry Finers for Harry Non-Twillers".)

All university journalism is ephemeral. Magazines come and go and there is no time to build up a big readership. Berry found he had to do some work for his finals and offered to hand over Parson's Pleasure to Paul and myself, who had been contributing occasionally to its pages. We were delighted, but soon found that it was not going to be plain sailing. For a start, there was the problem of getting advertising, no easy task when the circulation was only a few hundred copies.

The situation was saved in the end by Paul's uncle Michael who booked a regular full-page ad. for Tribune, of which he was then the editor. Paul told me later that Michael Foot paid for the ads out of his own pocket, a typically generous gesture on his part which served to help launch us both in our careers in journalism.

I met Michael Foot only once during those years, when Paul took me to a party his uncle and his wife Jill gave in their cottage on Lord Beaverbrook's estate. Paul saw more of his aunts and uncles than he did of his parents, especially in the years when his father, Hugh, was the Governor of Cyprus, then fighting for its independence. Hugh Foot came to Oxford once or twice and later I came to know and love him – a stocky figure with bushy eyebrows, a trace of a Cornish accent and an apparently inexhaustible supply of optimism about the human race. Paul mocked him in a most affectionate way and we cherished certain favourite stories about him. One of those involved him walking through St James's Park after an unproductive meeting at Downing Street with Harold Wilson and his ministers. Overcome with anger and frustration he shouted "It is INTOLERABLE!" so loudly that all the ducks flew up in alarm.

I always remember him taking Paul and me out

to lunch in Soho and the conversation turning, as it so often did, to the Middle East situation. As a former colonial officer in Palestine, this was a special concern of Hugh Foot. He was a lifelong supporter of the Palestinians and, in his role as UN Ambassador, the man mainly responsible for the passing of the famous resolution 242 calling for the Israeli withdrawal from all the territory captured in the war of 1967. Suddenly he turned to me across the table, "And what's your view?" I stammered something to the effect that there were points to be made for both sides. "That's the easiest thing in the world to say," he snapped back. He was quite right of course and in the end I came to share his sympathy for the Palestinian people – one of the few questions on which Paul and his father were in complete agreement.

Both of us ended up being dubbed anti-semites and this charge was regularly hurled at Private Eye, in particular by three most persistent, and in my view, paranoid critics – Harold Pinter, Kenneth Tynan and Jonathan Miller. The same was later alleged by Marcia Williams (Lady Falkender) who used it as justification for Goldsmith's assault on the Eye. Neither Falkender nor Wilson could deny that they were beholden to a number of rich Zionists, including the infamous Lord Kagan, and that this alliance was responsible for the fact that Hugh Foot was not re-appointed to the United Nations job when Wilson returned to power in 1974, being replaced by the Jewish lawyer Ivor Richard.

Paul's favourite uncle was John Foot who lived with his American wife Anne on the edge of Dartmoor at Crapstone near Yelverton. John Foot was a clever, successful solicitor with a practice in Plymouth and an active Liberal whose dry wit greatly appealed to Paul. He loved to repeat what his uncle had said once to his wife when she forgot to lay the knives and forks for dinner, "How are we supposed to eat this, Annie? Throw it up in the air and catch it in our mouths?".

In the summer of 1959 I drove with Paul in his old Jowett car to visit his West Country relations – a major trek in the days before the motorways. We spent a day or two with his grandfather Isaac before going on to John's. Isaac Foot, the patriarch of his extraordinary family, was seventy-nine and still living in a large house, Pencrebar, three miles out of Callington in Cornwall. Isaac had been a Liberal MP and briefly a junior minister in the National Government of 1931. He was a Methodist lay preacher and a leading figure in the Temperance movement, so there was no alcohol in the house. When Paul and I went for a drink to a local pub in the evening Paul would say to his grandfather, "We're just going to look at a church, grandpa". The old man would nod his approval.

In the evening after supper he asked Paul to read out some of his old speeches in Parliament. "Louder! Louder!" he insisted. Like Michael, and later Paul, Isaac Foot was a bibliophile though, in his case, it was more like a mania. The whole house was crammed with books (70,000 in all) with one whole room devoted to scores of different editions of the Greek Testament. Isaac was teaching himself Greek in order to read the Gospels in the original. He was also struggling to learn the piano, having developed in his old age a passion for Bach. When he found that I could play, he insisted on my having a go at some of the Preludes and Fugues. His enthusiasms, his passion for books and oratory had obviously inspired his son Michael especially, and also Paul, who remembered how, when he was a boy, the old man had paid him half a crown for learning Macaulay's poem Horatius by heart.

As far as Isaac's library went, I don't remember that either of us expressed any special interest in his collection of Greek Testaments. We were more excited to discover in an upstairs room the rare first edition of Lady Chatterley's Lover still banned in England at that time. We were poring over this late one morning in the bedroom that we shared when Isaac came in and announced to Paul, "Now, my boy, you have to drive me into Liskeard. You have half an hour for prayer and meditation".

In the meantime, we went to pubs and did actually visit some churches (Betjeman's guide to parish churches had just been published). When it was hot we would go swimming in the river on Dartmoor. "I would always take a book," Paul remembered. "The summer of '59 was absolutely wonderful and we would sit on Cornish cliffs or the hills of Bodmin Moor." He was amazed how I was able to sit for hours without doing anything, whereas he had to be active, talking or reading a book. He put this down to my religious side, but indolence was probably a more plausible explanation. Whatever the truth, he was attracted to my contemplative nature as I was to his industry and enthusiasm. He gave me politics, I gave him music. We came together in journalism, which to begin with meant Parson's Pleasure.

Shortly after taking over the magazine we had our first libel action. On giving up the editorship Adrian Berry had asked us to publish something he had written in the next issue. "Close friendship," he wrote, "can easily degenerate into homosexuality and the relationship between X and Y [here he named two prominent undergraduates] has become so scandalous as to merit the attention of the authorities." There was no truth in the suggestion; it was just Adrian's idea of a joke and Paul and I, out of deference to our benefactor, put the article in without giving it a second thought. The next thing we knew was that the two named by Berry had instituted proceedings for libel. Luckily, as Berry's father owned the Daily Telegraph, he was able to pay them off.

We produced Parson's Pleasure for two terms before the financial situation became impossible. Paul wrote reviews of Oxford Union debates, in which he had become involved, while I supplied parodies and occasional drama criticism. We built up a little gang of helpers and would lunch regularly at a greasy spoon cafe called the Town and Gown, down an alleyway off the High. Regular attenders were Noel Picarda, an army friend of Paul's, Candida Betjeman (another groupie whose loyalties were torn between us and the Christ Church toffs) and Andrew Osmond, a smartly dressed old Harrovian and ex-Ghurka officer. Sometimes at weekends we would be joined by Willie Rushton who, having done his National Service in the ranks, was working in a solicitors' office in London. We relied on him to supply the occasional cartoon, my favourite being a giraffe standing at a bar with the caption "The highballs are on me".

Gossip, which had been the mainstay of the magazine under Adrian Berry, was more difficult to come by, as none of us were in the smart party circuit. But I discovered that the readers were in the same situation and that a gossip column can therefore create its own celebrities. We proved the point by inventing a completely fictitious undergraduate called Susanna Harcourt, newly arrived at St Anne's, who was written up as a kind of Zuleika Dobson figure, extraordinarily beautiful, courted by the blades and invited to all their drinks parties. The joke was so successful that, as time went on, I began to meet people who claimed to have dated her.

In our final year I retired to my digs at 99 Woodstock Road to try and catch up on the work I should have been doing in the first years. Paul, however, was not

"The highballs are on me"

to be cowed by the thought of looming finals and accepted the editorship of Isis, which had recently been taken over by the wealthy Christ Church undergraduate David Dimbleby, who expelled all the New Leftists and did his best to make the magazine more mainstream.

Paul got his first taste of national publicity when, as editor in succession to Dimbleby, he began to commission reviews of the dons' lectures, the chief reviewer being our fellow Univ man John Davis, who later became the Warden of All Souls – one of the most prestigious jobs in Oxford. Not long after the reviews started there were complaints that a philosophy don, Philippa Foot (wife of the historian MRD Foot), had been so upset by the hostile review of her lecture on "Explanation of Behaviour" that she had suffered some kind of nervous breakdown. The proctors, the university's private police force, then intervened and ordered a stop to the reviews, but not before Paul had achieved nationwide publicity by being interviewed on the BBC.

In his final term, Paul at last achieved his father's ambition for him and was elected President of the Oxford Union, traditionally a kind of nursery for would-be politicians. Paul may have had a vague idea of becoming an MP – he did once stand as a Socialist Worker candidate in 1977 – but he was perhaps more interested in simply following the family tradition. He was already a brilliant speaker partly because, as with anything he did, he worked very hard at it. Like his uncle Michael he first wrote out his speech and then learned it by heart, rehearsing in front of his bedroom mirror. With such care being devoted to delivery and timing he was naturally impatient with interrupters, a fact noted by the Isis critic (Lord Gowrie) who accused him of "a sharp intolerance" when dealing with hecklers. (First interruption, "Will you please stop interrupting". Second interruption, "Stop blathering".)

Partly because of the length of the debates which often went on until 11 at night, I never got involved in the Union, apart from occasionally helping Paul with carefully rehearsed interruptions. He did however invite me, along with Andrew Osmond, to be one of the tellers (vote counters) at his farewell debate where one of the speakers was Malcolm Muggeridge, at the time a hero with rebellious students like us on account of his attacks on Winston Churchill and what he called "the Royal Soap Opera". When Paul introduced me to Muggeridge he explained that I was working hard for my finals. Malcolm said in his familiar, much-imitated drawl, "The thing to remember, dear boy, is that no one in later life is going to be remotely interested in what class of degree you get". It was a very comforting piece of advice, as well as being perfectly true.

During my final term, as exams loomed, I was sometimes kept awake at night by the drone of voices in the room above mine, occupied by a post-graduate philosophy student at Univ called Colwyn Williamson. At one stage I became so frantic that I even thumped on the ceiling with a broom handle. It was only later that I discovered that Williamson's nocturnal visitor was none other than Paul Foot and that he was being tutored in Marxism by my fellow-lodger. Williamson had attracted Paul's attention first with an article on Marxism commissioned for Isis by Grey Gowrie (who took over the editorship from Paul). Later, Paul accosted Williamson with the question, "Is it true that you believe in collectivism rather than individualism?".

Despite my year's cramming, I succeeded in getting only a Third, whereas Paul got a second in Law.

We left Oxford and during the autumn of that year, 1961, the first rather desultory discussions were going on in various London pubs about starting the magazine which later turned out to be Private Eye.

Nothing much happened until Peter Usborne got involved. Usborne had already made his mark as a publishing tycoon in the making when he founded another short-lived Oxford magazine Mesopotamia to which both Paul and I contributed. It was a much glossier, more professional affair than Parson's Pleasure. One issue sported a hessian cover and a packet of mustard and cress seeds to grow on it and another had a gramophone record engraved on it – a technique later used by the Eye.

Having followed Paul's career at Oxford and admired his editorship of Isis, Usborne was keen that Paul should be editor of the new magazine. Paul was by now a working as a journalist on the Glasgow Record, thanks to Hugh Cudlipp, a friend of uncle Michael, and when I wrote to him at Usborne's request, he declined, explaining, "You see, Ditch [my family nickname], I'm part of a movement now".

It was true – having absorbed the message of Marxism at his nocturnal seminars with Colwyn Williamson, Paul was witnessing it in action in Glasgow, traditionally a focus of Socialist activity, with a thriving left-wing culture of old and New left, communists, anarchists and Trotskyists. Foremost among the latter was one Gus Macdonald engaged at the time in organising a strike of apprentices in the shipyards. Jean McCrindle, a member of the Glasgow Young Socialists, whose actor father, Alex, had been Jock in Dick Barton, harangued the workers from a soapbox on a corner of Sauchiehall Street and invited Paul to come down. "He watched for a while that evening," she wrote after his death. "He offered to speak the next Sunday, but he did have a weird haircut as well as a voice from his public school days. So Gus suggested that he get a new hairstyle, as Paul clearly couldn't do much about the accent, and that's how he came to have 'that hairstyle' which he never altered again. When he did get up on the soapbox the Glasgow working class audience undoubtedly noted his posh class accent but they

Paul at the Oxford Union — a caricature in Mesopotamia

did also admire his perseverance. It was not an easy thing for him to do, and he quickly adjusted his speaking style away from the Oxford Union, using his terrific wit and an unrivalled inside knowledge of his class to quieten the hecklers and impress the sceptical old lags who hung about listening." It was one such old lag who rebuked Paul when he later spoke about the danger of nuclear war breaking out by accident. "Comrade Foot must understand that wars are not caused by accident but by capitalism."

Paul took all the ribbing in good heart. The Scottish comrades showed little sympathy when he hung his jacket on a chair in a Glasgow pub, only to find that his wallet was stolen.

It was a tribute to Paul's great charm that his bourgeois habits never really jeopardised his political activities. Conversely, however, his political views occasionally led to tensions nearer to home. We all married young in those days and Paul was no exception, having got engaged to his Oxford sweetheart Monica Beckinsale shortly after coming down. Monica's parents were devout Catholics and were very upset when the young couple announced that they were going to get married in a Registry Office. In a solemn spirit of newly-found commitment, Paul explained his feelings to his mother-in-law to be:

"The trouble is that I CARE so much. I was brought up in a religious family. It is no purposeful thing – but as I have become deeply and passionately interested in politics and the relationship man has with society – I have simply found that where the Church has come into contact with politics, I have been on the other side. Also, in the last three months, when for the first time in my life I have come into contact with poor people and destitute people I have been horrified at the effect the Church can have upon them – horrified at the acceptance of dogmas, orders etc passed down by the Church (all the churches), I believe that people are entitled to things by right, not by bounty."

Like many idealists who reject religion, Paul took refuge in a political substitute with many of the same characteristics – sacred texts, small meetings of the faithful, the belief in a better world to come. I always thought of Paul's political activities as quasi-religious and therefore never saw the point of arguing with him, any more than he would have seen the point of arguing about my Christian beliefs, such as they were. I remember when I said how much I had enjoyed "A People's Tragedy", Orlando Figes' book on the Russian Revolution, he expressed a reluctance to read it, I suspect because he thought it might undermine his faith and especially his romantic idealised picture of Lenin and Trotsky.

In Glasgow in the early Sixties there was a variety of left-wing groups, but Paul was most taken with what was then known as the International Socialists (later re-named the Socialist Workers Party). Its leader was a Palestinian Jew, Tony Cliff (né Gluckstein), a charismatic individual, a brilliant speaker and (unlike most left-wing extremists) a man with a strong sense of humour. Gus Macdonald was another convert to I.S. but he was to fall by the wayside, disillusioned by the wearisome feuding than went on between the tiny bands of rival Trotskyists. Paul, to the puzzlement of his one-time comrades, remained faithful to the cause until his dying day – even if, by that stage, he had at last acknowledged that the hoped-for revolution was not going to happen in his lifetime.

While Paul was in Glasgow I myself was undergoing a political conversion of a kind, having taken over the editorship of Private Eye in 1963 from Christopher Booker. I found myself having to cope with a succession of political upheavals, notably the Profumo affair, the trial and suicide of Profumo's friend Stephen Ward, the society osteopath and the resignation of Harold Macmillan and his replacement by Lord Home, an appointment that caused widespread anger, especially at the Eye — so much so that Willie Rushton, by now famous on account of his appearance on the BBC's satire programme That Was the Week That Was, was persuaded against his better judgement to stand against Home (by now plain Sir Alec Douglas Home, having resigned his peerage and standing for Parliament in a by-election in Perthshire). The maverick publisher John Calder very generously offered his house at Ledlanet as our election headquarters, Bernard Levin wrote the election address and Mark Amory volunteered his services as agent.

It was the only time I saw Paul during his Glasgow years. Wearing his reporter's hat he attached himself to our campaign, acting as chauffeur for Willie and helping him to compose a fiery speech ridiculing Home and Macmillan. All in vain. Home was elected with a huge majority, Willie securing a mere 45 votes.

"I should say that in Glasgow it rains the WHOLE time," Paul wrote to his mother-in-law. "It rains EVERY day. And it is not just drizzle. It is real hard tropical cold rain which bites into you as you go along. I doubt whether I can stand it much longer." Whether or not the rain was responsible,

Paul returned to London in 1964 to join the staff of the new-look, short-lived Sun which was being launched by Hugh Cudlipp.

Copying the successful Sunday Times Insight feature – the work of a group of journalists engaged on 'in-depth' investigations – Cudlipp had formed a "Probe" team to do the same sort of thing. But Paul became disillusioned when having suggested a probe on capital punishment, the chief prober, who turned out to be a former Daily Express city editor, clapped his hands and said, "How much would we save by that? How much does an execution cost?".

After six months the whole probe team resigned and not long after the Sun was sold to Rupert Murdoch. Paul was offered a job on the recently launched Sunday Telegraph by its rather eccentric editor Donald McLachlan, a former Winchester schoolmaster and wartime Naval intelligence chief, remembered for wanting to appoint a blind man, T.E. Utley, as the paper's TV critic. Though one of nature's Tories he liked to have left-wingers writing in his paper.

One notable example was his columnist Claud Cockburn who, as a former member of the Communist Party, was still regarded with suspicion by most media potentates. In addition to his column at the Sunday Telegraph, Claud was closely involved with Private Eye. In 1963 I had persuaded him to come over from Ireland, where he had been living since 1947, to act as a guest editor for a single issue of the Eye which, as luck would have it, coincided with the trial and suicide of Stephen Ward. Claud's issue created a big stir, partly because he named the heads of MI5 and MI6 (I assumed always that he got the information from his great friend and former MI6 man Malcolm Muggeridge).

That particular revelation, we now know, was taken so seriously that the Prime Minister Harold Macmillan discussed with colleagues what should be done – in the end, nothing. But more important from the Eye's point of view was the story in Claud's guest issue of Harold Woolf, a 60-year-old artist who had died in suspicious circumstances after being arrested by the police. It was the first time the Eye had printed anything like this and it resulted in

Claud Cockburn

questions being asked in Parliament and eventually an official enquiry.

I took Paul round to meet Claud in his flat in Cornwall Gardens and was made at once aware of the great gulf that separated the Trotskyite and the Communist. Paul began enthusing to Claud about the Russian anarchist Victor Serge whose books he had been reading. Claud would have none of it. "Absolute rot!" he exploded to Paul's great disappointment. But as far as journalism went, the two were as one. The Hal Woolf story had proved one of Claud's maxims as passed on to Paul – "Listen to the loons", Mrs Woolf having previously trudged around Fleet Street with the story and having been dismissed as a nutcase. "What impressed me most about Claud," Paul wrote, "was the time he would spend with such people and how more often than not, they had more stories than had all the Reuters and AP tapes put together."

As his Sunday Telegraph job was part-time (three days a week), Paul was able to contribute to the Eye on a regular basis, Claud Cockburn having retired to his home in Ireland and now making only occasional visits to London. We began to form a team of helpers and informants. The Eye had already benefited from cartoonists whose work had been rejected by Punch, and the same sort of thing happened with the New Statesman, by now edited by the increasingly reactionary Paul Johnson. Peter Jay, who was working at the Treasury, became a regular visitor and Claud had put us in touch with a number of his old friends like Tom Driberg.

It must have been during this period that we started having regular lunches at the Coach and Horses, across the road from our office at 34 Greek Street, a tradition that has continued to the present day. Driberg was a regular attender though as one of nature's gourmets he objected to the rather basic food provided – steak and chips – and would insist on being served greens by the reluctant landlord, Norman Balon.

A Labour government, headed by Harold Wilson, took over in 1964 and Paul's energies were devoted to showing how Wilson in various ways was betraying the Socialist cause (he wrote a book on the subject 'The Politics of Harold Wilson (1968)').

It was a sign of how seriously the Eye was being taken as early as 1966 that an article by Paul on the Seamen's Strike of that year should cause serious concern in "official circles", as recently released papers now reveal. Wilson, in a typical move, had described the strike as being the work of a "tightly-knit group of politically motivated men" (i.e. Communists) on the executive of the National Union of Seamen. Proving that 'spin' is not a modern invention, Wilson now did his best to influence the press to follow up the story of a communist plot, offering papers evidence to confirm it.

The job of interviewing journalists was assigned to the Postmaster General George Wigg, Wilson's equivalent of Alastair Campbell, whose main job was to keep track of Ministers' private lives and thus prevent a Labour version of the Profumo affair. Paul's full page article headed "Tightnits in Observersmear" reported how attempts to interest the papers had failed with one important exception: the Observer (whose chairman the lawyer Arnold Goodman was closely involved with Wilson) had swallowed the bait and printed a huge article under the heading "The Plot Behind the Strike".

It is a tribute to Paul's journalistic skills that his article, published in a satirical magazine with a small circulation, had major repercussions. In a lengthy memo to Wilson, George Wigg detailed how he had been summoned by Lord Goodman to his flat, who impressed on him that the Eye's story had been written to discredit the Observer. Wigg proceeded to go through it paragraph by paragraph attempting to show how or from whom the Eye could have acquired this or that piece of information, concluding that the "Private Eye story was inspired by near-Communist sources".

Thus began an almost paranoid obsession toward Private Eye on the part of Wilson and his cronies. Tom Driberg was even convinced that George Wigg was keeping tabs on those who came to the Coach and Horses lunch with the help of a spy parked outside the pub. Wilson's long time aide Marcia Williams (later Lady Falkender) was so paranoid about the magazine that she ordered Wilson to sack the young Robin Butler (a contemporary of Paul's and mine at Univ) when she found that he had once been to the Eye lunch. Luckily for Robin, he was saved by the intervention of Bernard Donoghue, otherwise he might never have been able to pursue his distinguished career, ending as Secretary to the Cabinet and head of the Civil Service, life peer and Master of his old college at Oxford.

Wilson's obsession with the Eye was fuelled by his lawyer Arnold, later Lord Goodman, a large, shambling, rather sinister figure who, thanks to Wilson's patronage, had emerged from obscurity as a solicitor specialising in libel to become one of the most powerful figures in the country – chairman of the Observer and the Newspaper Proprietors

Arnold Goodman by Willie Rushton

Association, a special negotiator in Rhodesia and Chairman of the Arts Council. As such he was invariably sought out by politicians to keep embarrassing stories out of the papers.

Goodman was one of the few public figures ever to attempt to influence Paul. He was under attack from the Eye over his involvement in the sale of the British Lion film company and he rang

Paul up at home. Paul was initially convinced that it was me pulling his leg and told him to come off it, whereupon Goodman said that he was most concerned about the Hanratty case and intended to raise it in the House of Lords. Paul was summoned round to his flat where Goodman received him in his dressing gown. For a time it seemed that Goodman was genuinely concerned and he even drove out with Paul to see the spot near Taplow where the murderer had initially confronted his victims. But when the British Lion articles continued as before, his interest in the case faded as quickly as it had arisen in the first place.

Over the years Goodman conceived a vehement hatred of Private Eye and once refused to feature in a book of interviews by Naim Attallah when he discovered that I would be in it as well.

We had revenge of a sort when in 1971, at the height of the negotiations over Rhodesia, a fellow member of Paul's in the Socialist Workers Party, then working in Barclays Bank in the Strand, came across an internal memo showing that the bank was most concerned about an account in Goodman's name which was overdrawn to the tune of £20,000.

It did not seem such an interesting story, but Goodman's reaction showed that the Eye had inadvertently stumbled on a potential scandal.

Dropping everything, Goodman bombarded our lawyer Geoffrey Bindman with all manner of threats and eventually summoned all three of us round to his office, where he accused Paul and me of committing a criminal offence by printing the memo. When Geoffrey assured us that this was not the case, Goodman huffed: "I strongly advise you not to take the advice of your solicitor". As he continued to threaten, Paul remarked quietly during a lull, "Of course, Lord Goodman, you don't know what else we know". The fact was that we didn't know anything, but it was enough to stop him in his tracks and thereafter he proved more amenable.

It ended, as so often, with the Eye printing an apology. But after Goodman died it emerged that he had been stealing large sums of money from a trustee account that he held on behalf of a wealthy client, Lord Portman, and we assumed it was that which had accounted for Goodman's panic.

In February 1967, only a few months after the Tightnits article, Paul took a momentous decision – to work for Private Eye full-time. His family, especially his uncle Michael, were strongly opposed to the move and one can see why. Quite apart from the fall in salary involved, the Eye's future was uncertain, to put it mildly. After the initial craze for political satire subsided, the circulation fell and it was only thanks to Peter Cook, by now sole owner of the magazine, who injected not only money but jokes and ideas, that it had managed to survive. There had already been a number of libel actions, one brought by Lord Russell of Liverpool being particularly expensive.

In retrospect, it seems altogether astonishing that Paul was prepared to throw in his lot with us. When asked about it later he would say he could not resist the prospect of two whole pages with complete freedom to write whatever he liked. "I still recall the almost overwhelming sense of liberation," he wrote. "Off my back were the cloying hierarchies, the silly office intrigues and petty censorships which stifled so much writing in the official press." For this we both of us had to thank Peter Cook, a proprietor who never interfered and never even (until his final years) expected to be paid either as a contributor or a shareholder.

Paul always got on very well with Cook, only realising after his death how much the two had in common. "We both were born in the same week into the same sort of family. His father, like mine, was a colonial servant rushing round the world hauling down the imperial flag. Both fathers shipped

Paul with Peter Cook at a Private Eye Christmas lunch

their eldest sons back to public school education in England. We both spent our school holidays with popular aunts and uncles in the West Country."

Paul was always keen to dispel the idea of Peter Cook as one of nature's conservatives, remembering particularly how he had once agreed to give away the prizes at an Anti-Nazi League fête in North London. But then Paul was always eager to hail people he liked and admired as fellow-revolutionaries. The appeal of Peter Cook and the Eye as a whole was more fundamental, as he explained to Peter's biographer (and mine) Harry Thompson. "Peter was suspicious of rulers of every description, but in particular he detested the secrecy, pomposity and hypocrisy which sustains them. The point about Peter – and the point about Private Eye – is that they spotted a simple and very elementary fact, which is that the world we live in is run by hypocrites and humbugs who are mainly helping themselves to money which has been provided by someone else and then slapping themselves on the back for this brilliant achievement. Whatever his political approach, he recognised that the most powerful weapon to use against such people, the one that goes really deep into them, is mockery. Nothing hurts important humbugs more than the sound, the huge roar of the people laughing at their absurdities."

It was this laughter, not to be found in abundance either at the Sunday Telegraph or later at the Socialist Worker, that attracted Paul to Private Eye more than anything. Ensconced at 22 Greek Street, a no-frills office next to a betting shop and above a strip club, he liked to hear the roars of laughter in the next room where the jokes were being composed by the regular team of myself, Christopher Booker and Barry Fantoni, and occasionally Peter Cook. Down the road in the

Paul Foot at 22 Greek Street — cartoon by Barry Fantoni

Coach and Horses we had a table regularly reserved for the Eye at lunchtime and would-be contributors knew they could find us there most days. A gang had been created, the essential basis for any successful magazine.

The fact that the Private Eye gang held together, with various comings and goings over the years, was not really due to any great unity of purpose, but more to the mundane fact that working for the editorial part of the magazine was never a full-time job. We worked alternate weeks, so although Paul might describe himself as full time, he had plenty of time to do other things.

He was already engaged in what was to preoccupy him throughout his life, the A6 murder for which James Hanratty had been executed in 1962. It was the first of those miscarriages of justice which took up so much of his time over the years, involving a huge amount of work, meetings, protests and court cases. One of my enduring memories of staying with Paul and his second wife Rose in their flat off Finchley Road, was of peaceful evenings being punctuated by lengthy phonecalls from one or other of those victims of injustice – in the case of Hanratty, it could be his relatives, all of whom saw in Paul their one chance of redress, or Peter Alphon, the man who one minute confessed to being the murderer, but denied it the next.

Why was Paul prepared to give up so much time to these cases? Some people would have said that he wanted to expose the shortcomings of British justice and the corruption in the Police Force. That may have been the effect of his various campaigns – Hanratty, Bridgewater, Colin Wallace – but I think his motivation was simpler and more honourable, namely to help individuals, the Hanratty Family for example, who had been caught up in a system that they did not understand and which left them with a feeling of powerlessness.

"He would have made an outstanding lawyer," wrote our great friend Anthony Sampson, impressed, as I was, by Paul's capacity to immerse himself in the details of these cases. Our own forays into the law, however, were not always crowned with success.

In 1967, shortly after he joined the Eye's staff, we became involved in a comic libel action brought by two reporters in the People, Hugh Farmer and Denis Cassidy, at the insistence of their editor Bob Edwards, always referred to thereafter as "the silver- haired creep". Paul had written the story of how Stuart Christie, a Scottish anarchist imprisoned by the Spanish authorities for plotting to blow up General Franco, had, on his release, sold his story to the People. Farmer and Cassidy were put on the case and accompanied Christie back to his home city of Glasgow. The three men spent the night on the town, ending up in a brothel where Christie had sex with a prostitute at the People's expense.

As so often, it was one person's word against another (or, in this case, two others). The People journalists, however, produced a number of witnesses to back up their alibi for what had happened on the night in question. This involved a visit to a restaurant which they left when they found it to be full. Paul and I were jubilant when we discovered that the restaurant had in fact been closed. We also produced two men who had witnessed a conversation between Denis Cassidy and Stuart Christie a few days after the Eye published the story. According to them, Cassidy had been trying to persuade Christie to deny the article. Christie however maintained that Cassidy had been too drunk to witness anything, to which Cassidy had replied that "he wasn't so drunk as he didn't see Bollocky Bill here performing". It was the sort of evidence which would have satisfied any journalist but which, when recited in open court, was made to seem unreal and faintly improper.

The judge, Mr Justice Brabin, admitted that the journalists' evidence was "unsatisfactory", but nevertheless came down on their side and awarded them each £500 damages.

Mr Justice Brabin, I read later, was one of many legal luminaries who had conducted an official investigation into the case of Timothy Evans, hanged for the murder of his baby in 1949, though it was revealed later that his landlord John Christie had murdered the baby, Evans' wife and several other women as well. Brabin, however, somehow managed to satisfy himself that Evans had murdered his wife (for which he had never even been tried) and that therefore two murderers had, by a strange coincidence, been living independently in the same run-down little house in Rillington Place, Notting Hill.

It was a good example of the bizarre lengths to which judges would go to avoid admitting that there had been a miscarriage of justice – a factor that was to stand in the way of nearly all Paul's campaigns on behalf of innocent prisoners.

The strangest but perhaps the most important court case in which Paul and I were involved arose from his exposure in 1970 of the Poulson Affair. More than anything, this story established the Eye's reputation for printing stories that no one else would touch – though it was a curious fact that, as so often happened, when the story was first published no one took any notice of it.

In a three-page article headed "The Slicker of Wakefield", the longest he ever wrote, Paul outlined the basic facts: how an unknown Pontefract architect, John Poulson, had built up a huge business not just in England but all over the world by

REGGIECIDE 2

THE SLICKER
OF WAKEFIELD

(With apologies to Oliver T. Dan Goldsmith).

J G L POULSON

Revelations in the *Bradford Telegraph and Argus* of April 9 about property companies in Bradford, Pontefract and elsewhere have been studiously ignored by the national press, much to the relief of leading politicians of all parties. The article, however, has been handed to the Investigations Committee of the Royal Institute of British Architects and its disclosures could well cause some discomfort in circles not confined to

instance, the South Cheshire Hospital and the General Hospital at Gozo, Malta, both of which were built by Taylor Woodrow. Recently he designed a new extension for Southlands Hospital, Shoreham.

Southlands falls under the South West District of the Metropolitan Hospital Board, for which Mr Poulson has also designed a new kitchen and dining room at Worthing Hospital. The secretary of the Board is Mr E G Braithwaite, an old friend of Mr

1964, Dan Smith hurried from the North to hold himself (in his Mayfair flat) in readiness for a call from Downing Street. Eventually, however, he had to settle for the Chairmanship of the Northern Economic Planning Council.

Dan Smith himself had set up a number of public relations companies, which helped him in his work as link-man between developers and Labour local authorities.

enlisting the help of an army of corrupt councillors and politicians. Of these the most valuable to him by far had been the deputy leader of the Conservative Party Reginald Maudling, a clever, amiable but intensely greedy man who badgered Poulson for every penny he could get back for himself, his wife and his son Martin, in exchange for his services as a prestigious representative of the firm. In his quest for money, Maudling had become involved not just with one but two major crooks, the other being the American, Jerome Hoffman, whose Real Estate Fund of America had been engaged in a massive 'offshore fund' fraud. Maudling had lost to Edward Heath in the Tory leadership election of 1965, but he became the deputy leader and when the Tories were re-elected in 1970 he was appointed Home Secretary — an unfortunate move considering that he would inevitably be involved in decisions about the prosecution of his former business colleagues.

Paul had always stressed the way the lobby system, not just in politics but other fields as well, prevented information from reaching the public. A group of accredited correspondents formed into a lobby would be given privileged off-the-record briefings by politicians or, say, the police and thereby develop an over-cosy relationship.

In 1971 the lobby correspondent of the Observer was Nora Beloff who took a dim view of the Eye's revelations about Maudling and who, like many lobby journalists who knew him, regarded him with sympathy and affection. Unfortunately for Beloff, her colleagues on the Business section of

*Reginald Maudling –
cartoon by
Nicolas Bentley*

the paper, who did not know Maudling personally, took a different view and had decided to follow up the Eye's revelations about the Real Estate Fund of America. Alarmed at this development, Beloff wrote a long memo to her editor and the owner of the Observer, the multi-millionaire the Hon David Astor, a man of admired liberal views who was said once to have held up an editorial conference at the paper by asking "What is a mortgage?".

"I had an interesting talk with William Whitelaw," she wrote, "who drove me back from the Carlton Club to the House of Commons. I told him the young Tory I had been lunching with and I had been speculating about who would take over if the PM ran under a bus. He said instantly that there was no doubt at all that it would be Reggie Maudling...

"I asked him about the Private Eye campaign and he conceded that in Maudling's place he probably already would have sued. He did not, however, think the campaign had damaged Maudling, as he thought Private Eye had over-reached itself and lied on so many subjects about which everyone knew...

"What I would like to suggest is that I do a study of Maudling instead of my usual political notebook. If you agree, I will very carefully look at the evidence accumulated against Maudling by the Private Eye people on the business side and confront him frankly with the case to hear what he has to say..."

The business editor Anthony Bambridge was not happy with the idea, but Beloff was very close to David Astor and he duly agreed to her proposal. Beloff went ahead with the long profile which was, as had been predicted, full of mistakes. Angry at being by-passed, Bambridge leaked her memo to Paul who printed it *in toto* alongside a catalogue of all the errors in the defence of Maudling.

It was difficult for Beloff to sue for libel so, on the advice of her lawyers Oswald Hickson Collier (led by the infamous Peter Carter Ruck), she brought an action for breach of copyright over the re-printed memo, even though technically the Observer owned the copyright and she had first to persuade David Astor to assign it to her.

Astor supported her litigation financially, an extraordinary thing for a liberal newspaper editor to do, considering that papers, including his own, were regularly printing leaked confidential memos and documents. Indeed it was not difficult for the Eye to find examples of the Observer doing precisely that. Astor, however, confirmed his liberal credentials by allowing the anti-Beloff faction on the Observer, which included her rival Anthony

Howard, to give evidence in support of Private Eye. Astor himself gave evidence for Beloff; it was the only time I saw him and I remember how he seemed to writhe in the witness box as if in pain caused by having to twist the truth.

Paul and I both gave evidence in a case which lasted for eight days, four of which were taken up with Beloff's counsel, Mervyn Davies QC, addressing the judge on copyright law. In the end, Mr Justice Ungoed-Thomas sided with Private Eye and even went out of his way to commend Paul and myself, in contrast to David Astor. "Mr Ingrams and Mr Foot," he said, "were of a younger generation, very able and serious-minded, impatient with what they regarded as stuffiness or pomposity, sincere and truthful. Except on one or two rare occasions of no great significance... they were forthright and unrestrainedly outspoken, without hesitation even when they must inevitably have realised perfectly well that what they were saying was to their own disadvantage. There was nothing devious or muffled about them and any criticism must be of very opposite qualities. They were excellent witnesses." (I quote this in full, as it was I think the only occasion on which Paul and I were praised by a High Court Judge.)

Whatever his views on our performance in

the witness box, Judge Ungoed-Thomas really had no option but to come down on our side as, if Beloff had succeeded, it would have created a dire precedent which might have prevented newspapers in future from reproducing confidential documents from whatever source.

Beloff had revenge of a sort by winning a separate libel action against Auberon Waugh who, in his HP Sauce column, had claimed that she had slept with every single member of the Cabinet though, he added, "no impropriety occurred". Attempts to show that this was a joke, always a difficult thing to do in a Court of Law, failed and Beloff won the case*.

It did her little good, as she was savagely ridiculed by Bernard Levin in the Times and some time later when, at the age of 56 she married a sports writer on the Observer, Clifford Makins, Bron wrote in his diary, "If I had been best man, I would have given Clifford the advice I always give bridegrooms on these occasions: take things gently at first, there's no rush. A new bride should be treated like a new car. Keep her steady on the straight, watch out for warning lights on the ignition and lubrication panels, and when you reckon she's run in, give her all you've got."

---

* "In a British courtroom, an ordinary act like eating a sausage can be made, under cross-examination, to sound like some bizarre perversion" – Auberon Waugh.

Bron Waugh and Paul were mutual admirers and great friends – they later even shared an office at the Eye, a fact that surprised those people who believed and still believe that Left is Left and Right is Right and that never the twain shall meet. In fact, they had more in common than otherwise, most obviously in their suspicion of politicians, all of whom, in an often expressed view, Bron considered to be "social and emotional cripples".

There was also a family link. Bron had done his National Service in Cyprus where he had shot himself in the chest when climbing off an armoured car and very nearly died. Though they were in the thick of the Cyprus emergency, Paul's parents, installed in Government House, went out of their way to help – putting up Bron's mother when she flew out to visit her seriously-injured son. Later, Paul's mother Sylvia regularly visited him in hospital and read Lawrence Durrell's book "Bitter Lemons" to him (succeeding only in irritating him). She also expressed the hope that when he went up to Oxford he would get together with her son Paul.

In the event, the only contact they had there was once when Bron, who had heard a rumour that Parson's Pleasure was for sale, came round to Paul's room with his friend, Bobby Corbett. We knew

Bron Waugh posing as a distinguished diarist in the office he shared with Paul

Bron by repute as a typical Christ Church man, rude and snobbish, and treated him accordingly. In any case we had no intention of selling him the magazine. Throughout our brief meeting I sat with a cushion balanced on my head and we both laughed

The Foot family at Government House in Cyprus. (L to R) Paul, Sylvia and Hugh (parents), Benjamin and Oliver (brothers), and sister Sarah

The editors of Parson's Pleasure (and Brahms)

*A Mesopotamia spoof. Group includes John Wells (back row, right),
Richard Ingrams, Peter Usborne and Andrew Osmond (centre,
seated). Paul on ground*

*Paul at a Young Socialists gathering at Skegness with Gus
Macdonald, later Lord Macdonald of Tradeston, CBE*

Paul receiving What The Papers Say award from Harold Wilson 1972

*CRICKET MATCHES AT
ALDWORTH*

*Paul with baby son
Tom (above). With Fred
Ingrams (right)*

*The two teams 1980. Group includes Willie Rushton, Richard Ingrams,
Peter McKay, Jeremy Deedes and Nigel Dempster. Paul is third left
(kneeling)*

A rare shot of Paul in pensive mood (with son Matt)

Paul at Aldworth with his three sons (L to R) Tom, Matt and John

Paul with members of the Hanratty family

*Outside the
Law Courts*

*Book browsing
outside the
Festival Hall*

*Revisiting
Shrewsbury with
daughter Kate,
summer 2003*

scornfully when Bron announced that he wanted to make Parson's Pleasure "the organ of the bloodies".

After that meeting I always regarded Bron with suspicion and was surprised when in 1968 he wrote an article in the Spectator, listing a number of people, including me, whom he said should be given an honour. This led to our meeting and shortly afterwards Bron joined the Eye as political correspondent.

He never quite fitted into the gang, avoiding the Coach and Horses at lunchtime in preference to the Beefsteak Club, but he was always devoted to Paul, later writing in his memoirs that "Sanctity attached to Paul Foot as the only left-winger on the staff. He was the moral justification for all our confusion of unharmonious responses to the modern world. We all sought his approval, as if he had been a beautiful girl. But he bore the burden lightly. Neither he nor Ingrams seems to have changed at all over the years. For those who find it hard to understand how anyone can claim to believe in workers' power without being a fool or a rogue, I produce Footy as my first exhibit. He is clever and funny and kind. Obviously there is a screw loose somewhere, but we all have our oddities. Ingrams doesn't drink, Rushton can't wear a tie. I would myself own up to a slight weakness for orientals."

Paul left the Eye in 1972 to become editor of the Socialist Worker. It was said at the time that he and I had fallen out over political issues. In fact, we very seldom disagreed about such things, the only tension arising from Paul's belief that whenever there was a strike he had to support the union regardless of any rights or wrongs. He also objected to a proposed cover showing his friend, the then pregnant revolutionary Irish nationalist politician Bernadette Devlin, talking to Harold Wilson (Wilson: Why are you going to call it Harold? Devlin: Because he's a little bastard). I dropped the cover after Paul's protest but learned later that, typically, Devlin had found the joke quite funny.

There were other things that upset Paul, like the cover featuring the black American revolutionary, Angela Davis. "I just couldn't bear these attacks," he told Harry Thompson later, but added, "It was terrible to leave. Their laughter was so infectious. In many ways it was the most uncomfortable decision I've ever made in my life. I felt I was abandoning Richard. I did feel a sense in which I was deserting my friend. He obviously felt that. He was very shaken."

A more cogent reason for Paul's departure in 1972 was that, like many left-wing Socialists, he

The Private Eye cover that never was

had begun to think that there might, after all, be a revolution in Britain. This was not as far fetched as it might seem now, as there was a deteriorating economic situation, frequent strikes by increasingly powerful unions, and a Tory Government headed by Edward Heath, apparently set on confrontation with the workers. 1972, he wrote in retrospect, was "the most tempestuous year of the post-war period during which every Tory policy and strategy was revised, not by parliamentary opposition, but by the actions of organised workers". It all amounted to what he called "an unparalleled blossoming of democracy".

In the meantime, we still saw a lot of each other. Paul continued to contribute the occasional piece and pay regular visits to the Coach and Horses. It must have been about this time that he began to develop symptoms of the bibliomania, or book-collecting disease, that ran in his family and I myself was showing signs of the same sickness.

After lunch we would make forays to Charing Cross Road or the book barrow at Berwick Street Market where all the books cost 20p, though later, to Paul's distress, they went up to 35p, an increase he blamed on Sir Geoffrey Howe, the Tory Chancellor of the Exchequer at the time. Even at 35p he was especially pleased to acquire "Where

Stands Socialism Today?" – a collection of lectures given to the Fabian Society in 1932.

Another favourite haunt was Cecil Court, the narrow pedestrian alley between Charing Cross Road and St Martin's Lane which had been appropriated by second-hand booksellers. We were following in the footsteps of uncle Michael, and Paul was greeted as one of the family by booksellers like the genial Robert Chris who sported a cardboard notice "Do not mistake my courtesy as an invitation to stay all day". I was collecting G.K. Chesterton and Beachcomber, Paul's main interest was his collection of the Left Book Club, a vast assortment of mostly unreadable tracts published in the 1930s by the crusading Victor Gollancz and bound in pink boards or thick orange cloth, easily recognisable on the shelves.

We and our wives went to concerts together – there was one memorable outing to the Three Choirs Festival in Worcester where we saw the Australians playing cricket in the afternoon and later listened to Hugh Bean playing Elgar's Violin Concerto in the cathedral with Sir Adrian Boult conducting.

Ever since Shrewsbury, Paul had been a keen cricketer and played regularly in our annual fixture, Lord Gnome's XI versus my home village team of Aldworth. A stylish batsman, he often partnered the equally stylish Peter Jay. In his history of this fixture, which lasted for 21 years, the long-serving Aldworth secretary and scorer, Bob Coles, records that in 1969 "Paul Foot made his name by scoring 67 of the 155 in reply to Aldworth's 167 of which Charlie Weaver hit 94 against Michael Parkinson's marathon bowl who finished with 6 for 91 off 13 overs". Michael Parkinson was only one of the famous names in Bob Coles' record. Others included Jonathan Routh, Willie Rushton (our original captain) and Roy Kinnear. One year Douglas Bader umpired for a few overs, though the regular umpire was the landlord of the Coach and Horses in Greek Street, Norman Balon, whose knowledge of the laws of cricket was distinctly sketchy and remained so throughout the years.

In later years, when cricket had become too strenuous, Paul developed a passion for golf – a distinctly bourgeois pastime – which I did not share and which gave rise to a great deal of good-natured mockery from journalist colleagues.

Left-wingers like Paul were not the only ones to feel elated by the chaotic political atmosphere of the Seventies. There were plenty of people on the Right, too, whose political ambitions were given hope during this strange period. There has never been a shortage of big businessmen who think they would be able to run the country better than the democratically-elected politicians.

Cecil King, the half-crazy owner of the Daily Mirror, had already talked about organising an anti-Wilson coup in 1968, while Sir James Goldsmith, like King an admirer of Oswald Mosley, made friends with Harold Wilson and his all powerful aide Marcia Williams and began to dream political dreams with himself as the man who would get things done.

Paul was not directly involved with the Eye when Goldsmith launched his massive libel campaign against the magazine in 1975. But this did not stop Goldsmith from identifying him as one of his main targets.

Goldsmith had purely selfish aims when he issued his barrage of writs: firstly, to stop Michael Gillard (Slicker) from investigating his shady business activities and, secondly, to curry favour with Harold Wilson and Marcia Williams, especially the latter, who had long been obsessed with the Eye and who was especially outraged by the recent revelation in the magazine that she was the mother of two children by the Daily Mail's political editor Walter Terry. But, to give a public-spirited gloss to

Wilson and Falkender — cartoon by John Kent

his campaign, Goldsmith formulated the idea of a Marxist plot to undermine the capitalist system, a sinister "cancer" spreading through the media, all of it linked to Private Eye. And a key figure in the conspiracy, possibly even its mastermind, was the notorious Trotskyite agitator Paul Foot.

Unfortunately for Goldsmith, his political plans were thwarted when Harold Wilson unexpectedly resigned in 1976 and when his peerage, one of the controversial nominations in what became known as Marcia's "Lavender List", was struck off by the Honours Scrutiny Committee.

Like all of us, Paul was obsessed by the story of Wilson's resignation and what lay behind it and at the Eye we even formed a special team, consisting of Paul, Michael Gillard and Patrick Marnham, to explore what Paul dubbed the country of "Wislonia" and get to the bottom of the resignation story. There were many possible angles – the slagheap scandal, involving the ill-fated land speculation engaged in by Marcia and her brother, the machinations of M15 who looked as if they had been bugging Wilson over his possible links with Russia, the band of mainly Jewish businessmen who had formed close links with Wilson and Marcia, one of whom, Lord Kagan, was to end up in prison while another, Sir Eric Miller, later committed suicide.

In the end, nothing of great significance emerged and it is now generally accepted that Wilson resigned for medical reasons, having convinced himself that he might inherit the Alzheimer's disease which had affected his mother and having decided, well in advance, that he would retire from politics at the age of 60.

He did indeed develop Alzheimer's and, in retrospect, it seems as if Wilson's mental capacities could have already been affected and could explain his rather strange behaviour before and after his resignation. Convinced that there was a multitude of conspirators working against him, in particular the South African intelligence services, Wilson summoned two freelance BBC reporters Barrie Penrose and Roger Courtiour, telling them, "I see myself as the big fat spider in the corner of the room. Sometimes I speak when I'm asleep. You should both listen. Occasionally when we meet I might tell you to go to the Charing Cross Road and kick a blind man standing on the corner. That blind man may tell you something, lead you somewhere" – possibly the most bizarre utterance ever made by a recently retired British Prime Minister.

The long-term effect of Wilson's move was not, as he had hoped, to expose South African saboteurs, but to revive the story of Jeremy Thorpe and eventually lead to his being brought to trial for conspiracy to murder his one-time lover, Norman Scott.

The Thorpe saga was a classic example of the kind of story at which Paul excelled. For a start, it confirmed his general belief that the more improbable a story is, the more likely it is to be true. To many journalists at the time it seemed an obvious fantasy, probably dreamed up in the unstable mind of Norman Scott. Others, like the then prestigious editor of the Sunday Times, Harold Evans, actually rallied to Thorpe's defence, believing that, as a gay, he was the victim of homophobic prejudice on the part of his persecutors. For the same sort of reasons, the comrades at the Socialist Worker

Acquittal of Jeremy Thorpe, July 1979

were not interested in what seemed to them an irrelevance. The only possible outlet for the story was Private Eye.

Paul tended to rely in his various campaigns on one key mole or informant with whom he would form a very close relationship. In the case of Thorpe, it was a producer for the BBC's Panorama, Gordon Carr, who himself had established an alliance with Det Supt Challes of the Avon and Somerset Police and the man in charge of the police investigation into the attempted murder of Scott. The regular flow of Footnotes, chronicling the slow progress of the police, undoubtedly kept the pot boiling in the face of press indifference and the strong official opposition from Thorpe's friends in high places who included, needless to say, Lord Goodman.

Paul's campaign culminated in an article "The Ditto Man" (Eye 433) which predicted the imminent arrest of Thorpe and his alleged fellow conspirators. After the months of investigations, Paul was naturally very excited. I remember him taking me for a walk through Covent Garden and telling me that Thorpe was about to be arrested and that he wanted to predict that this was what was going to happen. It is not every day that the leader of a political party is charged with conspiracy to murder, so any story to this effect was sensational, not to say fraught with

risk. But I had such faith in Paul's judgement that I had no qualms in publishing, though some readers, remembering our recent troubles with Goldsmith, were alarmed, especially when Thorpe issued a writ for libel, while his solicitor Sir David Napley (who had been ridiculed by Paul in an earlier article) sent a copy of "The Ditto Man" to the Director of Public Prosecutions for his immediate action.

The panic subsided when, two weeks later, Thorpe was indeed arrested. The subsequent trial at the Old Bailey attracted huge interest and was attended almost every day by Auberon Waugh who, like Paul, had become obsessed with the case which seemed to confirm his belief that there were no depths to which a politician would not sink in his quest for power.

In the end, Thorpe was acquitted, thanks to a friendly judge and the brilliant advocacy of George Carman who later became a friend of Paul's and a regular attender at the Eye lunch where he was invariably charming and indiscreet about those of his clients, like Mohammed Fayed, whom he did not care for.

The Thorpe story was only one example of the acuteness of Paul's journalistic instincts. What made him such an inspiring colleague and campaigner was his apparent ability to find all the news not only interesting but exciting.

I can remember watching News at Ten with him at Canfield Gardens and noticing how almost every item in even a dull bulletin seemed to give him inspiration – something that could be explored or followed up to see what lay behind it. It was the same with letters and phone calls at the office. Each and every one was of potential value, even if in the end they were found to lead nowhere.

After the Hanratty story, he had become a natural port of call for anyone who claimed he had been wrongly convicted of a crime. But he had always a very good instinct about such people. He would never have claimed to be infallible, but his overall record was outstanding. Good journalism must involve risk-taking, sticking your neck out and, in retrospect, it is sometimes hard to realise the degree of nerve it required to write some of these stories. In the case of high-profile murders or IRA bombings, the whole of the press, briefed by police or government spin doctors, would be saying one thing and to step out of line was to invite derision and disbelief. The most conspicuous example was Paul's long-running championship of Colin Wallace.

Wallace had been an information officer employed by the British Army at Lisburn, Northern Ireland, who in 1974 had taken part in an MI5 operation, code-named Clockwork Orange, aimed at discrediting the then Labour Government by suggesting that several ministers were supporters of the IRA. It was another example of the strange, unstable political atmosphere of the early 1970s which brought a number of wild right-wing elements to the surface, particularly in the intelligence services.

Wallace had been dismissed from the army when he refused to continue working for Clockwork Orange. He was subsequently convicted of killing his best friend (a conviction eventually overturned by the Court of Appeal). Like Claud Cockburn's Mrs Woolf, he had gone the round of Irish and British newspapers, trying, in vain, to interest them in his story and, like her, had been labelled "a nutter".

Almost the entire press, including very experienced Northern Ireland reporters like David McKittrick of the Independent and the BBC's John Ware, later swallowed the Government's propaganda that Wallace was a fantasist and a "Walter Mitty" (exactly the same label that was used some years later to discredit Dr David Kelly,

Colin Wallace outside the Law Courts with Paul's book

the Government scientist who tipped off the BBC about the way Tony Blair and his henchman Alastair Campbell "sexed-up" the dossier used to justify military action against Saddam Hussein).

As with the Thorpe saga, the Wallace story was, in any case, one that journalists steered clear of – the Left because they were suspicious of anyone who had worked for Army Intelligence, the Right because they were sympathetic to MI5. Paul was not only obeying Claud Cockburn's injunction to "listen to the nutters" but, more importantly from his point of view, to defend a man who had been let down by the system he believed in.

Colin had scarcely anything in common with Paul – he was an Army Officer, an Ulsterman, a natural conservative and, before his dismissal, a loyal and hard-working servant of the Establishment. It was to be another long-running campaign like Hanratty, ending with Paul's book "Who Framed Colin Wallace?" (1989), published in an unlikely alliance with the chairman of Macmillan, Lord Stockton (grandson of Harold Macmillan).

I remember Paul giving me an advance copy over lunch in Bianchis, Frith Street and joking that it could be a very rare book in future, as he was half-convinced that the Thatcher government would seek a court injunction to ban it. In the end nothing happened, and Wallace was eventually exonerated by Margaret Thatcher. But to this day the extraordinary story of how British Intelligence tried to undermine a democratically elected government in 1974 has never been officially investigated and probably never will be.

As the Seventies wore on and Wilson gave way to Callaghan and Callaghan to Thatcher, hopes of the revolution began to fade. Attempts were made by Paul and his ally Jim Nichol, who later became a solicitor and a major player in the Carl Bridgewater campaign, to widen the appeal of the Socialist Worker by including features on a broader selection of topics like feminism or football. But the comrades were not persuaded and Paul rejoined Private Eye in 1978.

I find it hard to recall the dates of his various comings and goings because there was never any animosity on either side and also because he never stopped contributing to the Eye, just as he continued to write a regular column for Socialist Worker until he died.

In the event he did not stay long on this occasion, being tempted away in 1979 by the editor of the Daily Mirror, Mike Molloy, who offered him a weekly "investigative" page of his own with only one condition attached: that he was not to make propaganda for the Socialist Workers Party. Though he was always dubbed an "investigative" journalist, Paul never liked the tag. "It's a complete fraud," he told Tony Harcup, who was researching a book on journalism, "The idea that there is a race apart called investigative journalists. It leads to hierarchical notions of grand journalists as opposed to less good ones."

Whatever his view, the move to the Mirror caused him a good deal of excitement. "On the day I went into the Mirror building in Holborn," he remembered, "and was shown into a little office on the fourth floor, I sat there all afternoon paralysed by delight and terror. Delight that such an unlikely dream had come true, terror as to how on earth I was to find the stories to fill the page."

Though he had not stayed long, that brief 1978-1979 period at the Eye had one important consequence, the launching of what was to be another of his lengthy campaigns – the Helen Smith story.

"I became fascinated," Paul wrote later, "in particular by people who were brought up to believe in God, Queen and Country, but who were treated shamelessly by all three." Colin Wallace was one, another was Ron Smith, a former Leeds policeman whose daughter Helen had gone to Saudi Arabia to work as a nurse and who died in mysterious circumstances at a drinks party in Jeddah in 1979, supposedly after falling 70 feet off the balcony of a flat.

The original story was submitted to the Eye by Jack Lundin, a freelance journalist then working in Jeddah, who met Ron Smith when he went out to Saudi Arabia to try to discover how his daughter had died. Paul took the story up and spent long hours with Ron Smith, both in person and on the phone; an arduous exercise, as Smith, like many of the victims of injustice, had become completely obsessed by his grievance. (Not for nothing did he describe himself as "a cantankerous bastard".)

One difficulty Paul experienced with "mainstream" editors was that they were easily persuaded that their readers would become bored with any form of long-running campaign. My own view was the exact opposite. I liked nothing more than a journalist like Paul banging on week after week about a particular story, and to hell with the readers.

He wrote regularly about Helen Smith for over two years in the Eye but, by 1981, the momentum had been lost. Ron Smith's demands for an inquest had been turned down and it was hard to see where we could go from there. It was then that I suggested that Paul should write a book about the story, in my experience the most likely thing to start things moving, partly because it brings together all the strands of a story that has been emerging piecemeal. Of course it is not enough to write a book, you have to ensure that people will read it. But here Paul was in his element, as he always set great store by being readable and, regardless of the issues raised, all his books – on Hanratty, Colin Wallace and Helen Smith – can be read by anyone who enjoys a good detective story.

But even when your readable book is written you have to find a publisher. And here we ran into difficulties. New English Library, a subsidiary of Hodders, was initially very keen and offered a huge advance. Paul wrote a synopsis which was received with rapture. But then the weeks passed and we heard nothing. Eventually, we were told that the managing director of NEL had vetoed the project. No explanation was given. Luckily, we were able to find a substitute in Collins' paperback division Fontana, though they were only able to give a more modest advance (most of which, I suspect, Paul gave to Ron Smith).

The resulting book, "The Helen Smith Story"

(1983), was another example of Paul's extraordinary attention to detail and his ability to master a complex story which, in this case, included a great deal of forensic testimony about Helen Smith's injuries.

Ron Smith's campaign, in which Paul and the Eye played a crucial role, had resulted eventually in a full scale inquest in Leeds in November 1982. From the evidence of the pathologists, it was fairly clear that Helen Smith had not fallen off the balcony, that she had been murdered and her body dumped on the street. To the distress of the authorities, the jury returned an open verdict, and the mystery of her death and the question of why the Foreign Office went to such great lengths to cover it up have never been explained.

Both Paul and Ron Smith were left with the feeling that there was one important element of the story which would explain it all but which had never been revealed. Paul himself remained convinced that the Foreign Office's behaviour had had something to do with a private visit to Saudi Arabia, coinciding with Helen's death, of HRH Princess Margaret. I am not sure who put this idea into his head, but it was a rumour he was never able to confirm.

Paul was to stay at the Daily Mirror for fourteen years, a remarkable feat considering that, five years after he joined, the paper was taken over by Robert Maxwell. Paul got a lot of stick about working for Maxwell, but his reply was always that he had secured a guarantee from the tycoon never to interfere with his copy. He also had the support of Richard Stott, who assumed the editorship in 1985 and who was a strong enough personality to protect his star columnist from the paper's bungling and crooked proprietor (whose right-hand man, by a strange twist of fate, was our old Oxford friend and Eye supporter, Peter Jay).

"On a glorious Guy Fawkes day in 1991," Paul wrote, "Maxwell was found dead in the sea after falling off his yacht near the Canary Islands." But the euphoria at the Mirror did not last long. A dour Ulsterman, David Montgomery, a former editor of the News of the World, organised a boardroom coup and embarked on a programme of union-bashings and sackings, the victims including the editor and Paul's defender, Richard Stott.

When Paul wrote a page attacking the sackings, the new editor, David Banks, refused to publish it and accused Paul of being out of his mind and in need of "professional help". Paul retaliated by printing his page as a pamphlet and handing it out in the street. But he was never going to work under Banks and was once again drawn back to the Eye.

This was in 1993 and things by then had changed. There was a new office at 6 Carlisle Street and a new editor, Ian Hislop. But Paul was no stranger to Ian, whom I had appointed editor in March 1986.

They had previously formed an alliance of sorts when I went on holiday in 1984, leaving Ian in charge. He found many of the Eye's regulars uncooperative and, in desperation, turned to Paul who was happy to assist and saved his bacon by sending in a plethora of pieces. There was even more antagonism towards Ian when I appointed him editor but Paul, who respected my judgement almost as much as I respected his, and knew also that I had had enough, rallied to Ian's defence. "My own feeling at the time," he wrote later, "was that anyone whom Richard thought worthy of the post deserved at least a chance."

He was of particular help to the magazine after Sonia Sutcliffe, wife of the Yorkshire Ripper, won her record damages of £600,000 in 1989. It was a classic instance of the unpredictable, lottery-like nature of the libel law.

A small item in the "Street of Shame" section

in 1981 had criticised various newspapers for practising chequebook journalism with Sutcliffe's relatives, following his conviction for murder. It never crossed anyone's mind to think that the article could be construed as defamatory of his wife. Nor did it appear to cross his wife's mind until some six years later when she was in financial difficulties and had discovered that you could win quite large tax-free sums in the libel courts.

Once again, the judiciary, in the person of Mr Justice Michael Davies, a man who achieved some notoriety later when he read out an apology to his car in court, failed to rise to the occasion, by failing to press Sonia Sutcliffe on the identity of the person from whom she had secured a £25,000 loan which had enabled her to hold on to her house when it looked as if she would be forced to sell it. Any fool could have realised that she must have got the money from a newspaper.

From the start, the Daily Mail had denied any dealings with Sonia Sutcliffe. It was Paul wearing his Daily Mirror hat who exposed the fact that the Mail on Sunday had paid her the £25,000 in a roundabout way via one of its reporters, Barbara Jones, in an attempt to avoid any charge of a direct payment. However, when the Eye introduced this new evidence in an appeal against the £600,000 damages, the Master of the Rolls Lord Donaldson ruled that it was irrelevant unless Mrs Sutcliffe was prepared to swear that she knew the money came from a newspaper. The damages were reduced, but this did not stop Sutcliffe from suing the News of the World

over another story. Thanks again to the brilliance of George Carman, who demolished her in the witness box by exposing the lies she had told in the Private Eye case, she lost and was left with a huge bill for costs equal, in all probability, to the money she had won in her previous actions.

Paul later wrote a pamphlet "Ripping Yarns", published by the Eye in 1991, which told the whole extraordinary saga. It was one of a series of such Eye 'specials' which showed once again his ability to tell a complex story in a readable and easily comprehensible style.

By 1993 the magazine had become more disciplined, more efficient, but inevitably some of the old camaraderie had gone. Paul had an office to himself and quickly adapted to the new routine and the new editor. "I found him a tougher editor than Richard," he wrote. "I had to fight for my stuff more strenuously than previously but it was none the worse for that." As for Ian, he recalls that when he took over he was naturally a bit nervous about dealing with Paul, a journalist much older and more experienced than himself. But when he ventured a few rather tentative criticisms of one of Paul's submissions, Paul simply said, "No problem", took the piece, crumpled it up and threw it in the bin. "Mind you," Ian adds, "it didn't stop him re-submitting it months later."

Although I had given up the editorship, I remained at the Eye as a member of the traditional joke-making team. Paul's office was on the second floor, along with the loo, which made it easy to drop in on him. However busy, he was always ready to chat.

People who met him for the first time either at Carlisle Street or at his home – he was by now living in Hackney with Clare Fermont – were sometimes surprised by the rather chaotic conditions in which he worked, his desk cluttered with letters, empty coffee cups and cuttings torn out of newspapers. They expected, perhaps, a team of researchers and a battery of buzzing computers. But he always had trouble with technology, finding it hard to master computers. His son John remembers Paul asking, when first introduced to a fax machine, how they managed to get the paper to go down the wire. Quite apart from that, according to John, he was late for appointments and "he always lost or mislaid normal items essential for everyday life, so often that the phrase 'keys, glasses, wallet' has become a family catchphrase".

He was able to function so well as a journalist because of his extraordinary powers of recall. He kept files of all his stories, but relied chiefly on what his one-time colleague Sarah Shannon called "an incredible memory for all the people he had spoken to over the years". According, again to John, he could reel off hundreds of telephone numbers, as well as remembering when and where he had bought almost all his second-hand books. Unlike me, he was able to recall practically every story he had written for Private Eye over the years, a particularly useful gift when so many villains had a habit of reappearing on the scene, hopeful that in the meantime he would have forgotten about their misdeeds.

If for whatever reason I missed Paul in the office, I saw him regularly at the Wednesday lunch, still at the Coach and Horses under the watching eye of Norman. Ian sat at the middle of the table, Francis Wheen at one end, Paul and I at what we dubbed the "old bores end".

"The Bohemian atmosphere of the Private Eye lunches," Anthony Sampson wrote after Paul's death, "provided his natural habitat, a relaxed setting where guests would lose their inhibitions and compete with stories and indiscretions." It was Anthony who, looking back on the media in his book "Who Runs This Place?", named the Eye as virtually the only paper to have survived unchanged since he published his famous "Anatomy of Britain" over forty years before in 1962.

Anthony, a quiet observer and outstanding journalist who managed to pay court to the Establishment without losing his radical zeal, was a particular favourite of Paul's. Though the people he invited to the lunches, journalists and MPs for the most part, tended to be on the left, he was never averse to Tories, partly because he liked to argue with them. The maverick MP Richard Shepherd was a regular, as was Ian Gilmour. Alan Clark came many times and Paul even invited Margaret Thatcher, when she was in opposition, to

Paul with Anthony Sampson at a Private Eye party

a couple lunches after they met on the BBC's Any Questions? But following New Labour's triumph in 1997, he frequently lamented the lack of informants in the party and it was noticeable how many more Lib Dems were invited in the years that followed. Sampson watched Paul "scribbling notes, not on a reporter's notebook, but all round a crumpled brown envelope which he pulled out from his pocket. It was disarmingly amateurish, but the answers were there".

It was always fun for me to watch newcomers to the lunch succumbing to Paul's overpowering charm. Not knowing him, they had sat down perhaps with some trepidation, expecting to be subjected to a form of Marxist inquisition. Instead they found themselves being drawn towards a smiling, even genial figure, who didn't look as if he could hurt a fly. This was not a façade because Paul was a genuinely benevolent person who was often loath to meet any of his potential victims because he was afraid he might like them too much – a feeling which to some extent I shared.

I had been writing a column for the Observer since 1987 and Paul was always a great help to me, just by acting as a sounding board. Writing a column is sometimes a little bit like driving in the fast lane. You zoom along quite happily at 90 or 100 mph until you are struck by a sudden awareness of what you are doing and succumb to momentary panic. Quite often as a columnist I would get the same sort of feeling – what on earth am I doing sounding off in public on issues I know nothing about? How long would it be before I was exposed as a complete fraud? It was always reassuring to find that Paul was generally in agreement with me on a great many stories – in particular the long-running saga of Northern Ireland which threw up so many scandals like Stalker (the Manchester deputy police chief dismissed when he tried to expose the RUC's shoot-to-kill policy), or the wrongful imprisonment of the Guildford Four and the Birmingham Six.

He always insisted there was nothing out of the ordinary in what he did, no special 'investigative' role. It was more to do with an attitude of mind. "Whatever you see," he told an interviewer, "there's a story behind it." Claud Cockburn had put the thing very well in his memoirs: "To hear people talking about facts you would think that they lay about like pieces of gold ore in the Yukon days waiting to be picked up – arduously, it is true, but still definitely and visibly by strenuous prospectors whose subsequent problem is only to get them to market. Such a view is evidently and dangerously naive. There are no such facts. Or if there are they are meaningless and entirely ineffective: they might, in fact, just as well not be lying about at all until the prospector – the journalist – puts them in relation with other facts: presents them in other words. Then they become as much a part of a pattern created by him as if he were writing a novel."

The gossip columnist Peter McKay who worked at the Eye on and off with Paul (and also at the Daily Mirror) put it another way: "First I decide what the story is and then I shepherd the facts towards it," adding, with a slightly melancholy air, "sometimes the facts are pitifully few."

Paul was not just a sounding board. I unashamedly relied on his campaigns when short of something to write about in my column.

A few months before he died, we both spoke about the Eye at the City of London University, at the invitation of our friend, the Professor of History, Peter Hennessy. Looking back at all his stories, Paul singled out two as being of special significance to him. One was a long-forgotten (by me) attack on Sir Arnold Hall, chairman of aircraft manufacturers Hawker Siddeley. The other was the Lockerbie air crash of 1988, which inspired another of his long-running campaigns and another of his special pamphlets published by Private Eye. It was a further case of Paul coming to the aid of a group of people (in this case the relatives of the Lockerbie victims) who found themselves, like Ron Smith, being fobbed

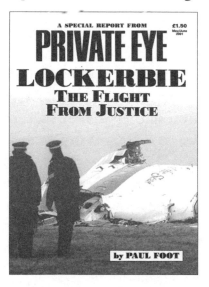

off by deceitful civil servants and politicians. It was also a case where the press and, in particular, the Sunday Times dutifully printed what they were told. The story they gave their readers was that the explosion of Pan Am flight 103 over Scotland had been instigated by Palestinian terrorists in the pay of the Iranians, in revenge for the blowing up of an Iranian airbus over the Persian Gulf. Then, when it became expedient to have Iran on side for the invasion of Iraq in 1990, the story changed and Libya for the first time was blamed. Again, the press fell into line, quoting unnamed security sources blaming agents of Colonel Gadaffi for the bombing. This story persisted and eventually, in 2000, two Libyans were charged by a Scottish court sitting in Holland, one of whom, Abdelbasset Megrahi, is still serving a 27-year sentence in a Glasgow prison. Gadaffi quite cynically paid up millions to compensate the families, as the price of getting sanctions lifted. Ever since, it has been accepted by the press and the world at large that the Libyans were responsible.

"Justice must not only be done, it must be seen to be believed" (Beachcomber). After all his experience of the libel courts and miscarriages of justice, Paul was unable to share the confidence of leader writers that justice had been done and the guilty punished. At the heart of the official version of events accepted by the judges and the press was a highly improbable story. Relying partly on the evidence of a humble Maltese shopkeeper who claimed to be able to identify a Libyan who bought a tee shirt from him twelve years previously, the judges accepted that a bomb in an unaccompanied case had been loaded onto a plane from Malta to Frankfurt, then transferred to Heathrow where it was put on a third plane bound for America, on which it duly exploded, killing 259 people.

Paul was always grateful for my echoing his opinions in the Observer, if only because nobody else was.

In this respect nothing much had changed since the Poulson days when his lengthy exposure of the architect had been totally ignored when first published in Private Eye. More than thirty years later, in 2002, Paul revealed how the Inland Revenue, under its chairman Sir Nicholas Montagu, had sold off all its properties to an offshore tax haven company in the Bahamas called Mapeley. It was obviously a major scoop, but no one took much notice. For once I was able to repay my debt to Paul, by drawing attention in my column to the way the story, like Poulson, had been ignored. There was an immediate flurry of interest from the press and TV.

On Easter Day, 15 April 1999, I was rung by Clare to say that Paul had been taken to hospital with a suspected heart attack, and that while in hospital his aorta had burst (a thoracic aortic aneurysm, to give it its full title). A five-hour operation had ensued and the aorta was repaired, but the doctors were pessimistic about his recovery.

A few days later I visited him in the London Chest Hospital in Bethnal Green. He was lying with his eyes closed and with all kinds of tubes attached to him. I could only sit by the bedside and say a few silent prayers. But the prospects were not good. During that first week, to add to an already desperate situation, his kidneys failed and he developed pneumonia. The head of the Intensive Care Unit summoned Clare and his sons and told them he thought Paul had suffered brain damage and could only survive in a vegetative state. It was what everyone had been dreading.

In the meantime there was nothing we could do except to wait and pray. I continued to trek out to Bethnal Green along with other friends. Then one day, a few weeks later, I went with Francis Wheen and Sarah Shannon, who worked with Paul at the Eye and who was deeply upset to see him in such a state. But I noticed that his eyes were open and that sometimes he smiled as Francis chattered away about the things that were going on.

That same evening I had a call from Peter Jay who had visited the hospital later in the day. He said he had been doing a one-person conversation, which was what we all did and, rather desperate for things to talk about, he began to tell a favourite story from their Oxford days about when he and Paul had been to see a film in Abingdon At the end of the film, as was customary in those days, the National Anthem was played. They both remained seated, whereupon a lady sitting behind them started to harangue them for their rudeness. To which Jay very typically replied, "Madam, as I believe neither in God nor the Queen..." He had got this far when, to his surprise, Paul completed the quotation from his hospital bed, "what is the point of calling on one to save the other."

From then on he gradually stopped hallucinating and slowly returned to normality. They moved him into a general ward at Homerton Hospital. Conditions there were not ideal, and Tariq Ali was so outraged by what he considered the neglect of Paul that he wrote to the consultant telling him who his patient was and suggesting that he deserved better treatment. It was the kind of interference Paul would have deplored, but he reaped the benefits when the staff began to pay him more attention.

A year or so later in an article in the Times (11 May 2000) Tom Stuttaford, who had spoken at length to Paul at an Eye lunch, wrote an article headed "Miracle of Writer's Unimpaired Intellect" (the use of the word "miracle" probably annoyed Paul almost as much at Tariq's behaviour). "The miracle," he wrote, "is that his intellect is unimpaired and his sense of humour as sharp as ever." Stuttaford described how, some time prior to his heart attack, Paul, who was worried about loss of memory, had had an MRI scan which showed his brain "to be in excellent shape", adding, "the pity is that the scan did not continue further down because the reason for his troubles would then have been evident."

Gradually his mental powers were restored, and it was not long before he was reading and even sending pieces into the Eye. (I remember sending him Martyn Gregory's brilliant book on the death of Princess Diana, which he reviewed with his usual skill for the Oldie.) But the hospital doctors, whom he had proved wrong over his mental powers, were still pessimistic about his chances of ever walking again. Here again Paul was to prove them wrong. In scenes reminiscent of the famous film about Douglas Bader, "Reach for the Sky", Paul was soon on his feet, clutching parallel bars and staggering slowly forward.

Once or twice that summer I went with Bron Waugh and Francis Wheen to see him in the evening and we wheeled him out of the hospital to a Vietnamese restaurant just round the corner. It was wonderful to see him back to his old form, gossiping and attacking New Labour while we divided up a roast duck between us. He told us that Tony Blair had visited the Homerton Hospital to launch one of his many NHS initiatives, but he had refrained from attending the press conference – a sign perhaps of a new feeling of benevolence.

At last, at the beginning of October, he returned home to Clare and his little daughter Kate. The following month he came back to Private Eye to general rejoicing. He was not able to work such long hours, but his enthusiasm and his curiosity seemed unimpaired, and it was during this final period that he produced two 'specials' – one on the Inland Revenue, another on the scandal of the Public Finance Initiative, both instances of his ability to explain a complex story in a simple, readable narrative.

I saw more of him during those last five years than ever. My office at the Oldie was in Newman Street, a few minutes walk from the Eye on the other side of Oxford Street. We took to lunching regularly at the Star Cafe in Great Chapel Street, whose proprietor Mario had always been devoted to Paul. Though by no means a gourmet's paradise – Tariq Ali was appalled when I took him there after Paul's death – it is a cheap and cheerful venue with large windows and lots of light.

Doctor Johnson, always so good at describing what life is like, once said that "the world has fewer greater pleasures than that which two friends enjoy, in tracing back at some distant time those transactions and events through which they have passed together". He could have been talking about Paul and myself, though I probably derived more pleasure than he did, as his memory of those transactions and events was so much better than mine. We had a great deal to talk about – school and university, the old battles in the Courts, books and music. But Paul was never a person to dwell much in the past. Apart from his work at the Eye and his fortnightly column in the Guardian, he was working hard to complete his last book, "The Vote", a massive historical survey of the struggle for universal franchise and the eventual betrayal of the voters by their elected representatives.

As it happened, I was also struggling with my long-deferred biography of William Cobbett, a man who had played a major role in the fight for political reform in the early decades of the nineteenth century. Paul shared my love of Cobbett, though he could not see him in the round. He was never a good historian because, like many Marxists, his view of the past was a black and white one, a story of rich capitalist oppressors pitted in an unequal struggle against heroic radicals and revolutionaries. The humour and enjoyment he derived from friends from all sides of the political spectrum was never reflected in his historical writing. Cobbett, like another of his heroes, Orwell, was a very English mixture of radical and conservative. Paul saw only the radical, and Cobbett became an admirable but two-dimensional figure.

The thing he liked most about Cobbett was the way he moved gradually from Right to Left in opposition to the general trend. The same was true of Tony Benn, whom Paul attacked in his youth, but came to revere.

As for Paul himself, his Marxist faith remained undimmed. I have been told that when he was introduced to John Smith, then leader of the Labour Party, Smith said to him, "You and I have one thing in common – our views haven't changed for thirty years".

It was a puzzle to his old friends from Glasgow days, such as Gus Macdonald and Jean McCrindle, how Paul could have stayed faithful to the Socialist

Workers Party for all those years, even when it had become clear that the Revolution, like the Second Coming, was not going to materialise. For his part, Paul had long stopped worrying about what the comrades might think of his bourgeois habits (there had been a time when he kept away from good restaurants in case the Party heard about it). At the same time, he worried about the backsliders among his friends. He could smile about Gus Macdonald becoming a life peer and a government minister, but when fellow journalists showed signs of revisionism it upset him. Nick Cohen, my Observer colleague, supported the Anglo-American invasion of Iraq. This was terrible. Would Francis Wheen at Private Eye be influenced by his friend Christopher Hitchens, once a diehard man of the left, now a cheerleader for George Bush?

Paul was exceptionally brave, but he could not disguise the strains imposed on him. He could walk only slowly with the help of two sticks and he suffered from frequent back pain, which eventually led to yet another operation. He could no longer play golf or nip down to the Charing Cross Road bookshops. Somehow he remained his cheerful optimistic self, though he must have been aware that another heart attack was on the cards. That was certainly the view of his great friend, the former Mirror editor Richard

Stott. "I felt that he had a fatalistic approach," he wrote to me after Paul's death, "but told me he was philosophical and prepared for it. He seemed almost to be embracing it."

I had that same feeling, even though nothing was said – and having lost so many friends already, I was determined to see as much as possible of him.

Apart from our outings at the Star, we arranged a number of lunches at the Gay Hussar in Greek Street, favourite haunt of Uncle Michael and other old Labour stalwarts and, from the gourmet point of view, a cut above the Star. Richard Stott and Peter Jay came, the latter having to put up with a lot of teasing over his role as Robert Maxwell's right-hand man. Eva, widow of the historian A.J.P. Taylor, who loved Paul and who, as a historian, had studied the Chartists, was another of our guests, as was Michael Foot, still lucid and voluble at the age of 90. There was our old Eye colleague of many years, Michael Gillard, and Ronald Waterhouse, the magazine's libel reader in the early days, now a retired High Court judge. I introduced Paul to some of my friends, among them Robert Harris and Andrew Wilson, and in due course they became friends of his as well.

Perhaps his main disappointment during this final period was the decision of the Court of Appeal in May 2002 to uphold the conviction of James Hanratty.

After the exhumation of his body, hopes had been high that the DNA tests would finally exonerate him. But they did not. Such is the faith in DNA, a subject about which the public understands very little, that the verdict was considered unassailable and it was generally suggested that all the years Paul had spent campaigning for the dead man and his family seemed to have been wasted. He had simply got it wrong.

Paul would have been the first to admit that he was not infallible and did get things seriously wrong from time to time, as we all do. But after all those years he had very little faith left in the judicial process; as for the DNA, he had seen before in the case of the Birmingham Six, where a government scientist had stated categorically that the men had traces of explosive on their hands, that scientists could get it wrong just as badly as journalists. What was the history of the trial exhibits from which Hanratty's DNA had been taken? No one was alive to give evidence about it. More importantly, how could the Appeal Court judges explain away Hanratty's alibi, which Paul was satisfied he had established beyond any doubt? His critics however, unfamiliar with the details, were not really

Acquittal of the Bridgewater Three. Ann Whelan on the left

interested in such questions. At the mention of the magic formula DNA they accepted the verdict of the court without question, muttering insincere words of sympathy for Paul who had spent all those years on a misguided crusade.

As with so many of his stories, the truth remained elusive and probably will remain so. The same was happily not true of the Carl Bridgewater case. The three survivors convicted of the murder of the newspaper boy had been finally released in February 1997: it was perhaps Paul's proudest moment, and a framed picture of the freed men outside the Law Courts occupied pride of place in his office at the Eye.

In 2002, when we both reached the official retirement age of sixty-five, Paul was determined to celebrate the milestone with a party. In October a large gathering was convened at Simpson's-in-the-Strand, including family, friends from Oxford and journalism and old Eye supporters, some of whom we had not seen for many years. Paul made a speech of which I can remember little except that he recalled I had insulted him at the Shrewsbury Debating Society – "Most of the people in this country are weeds. P. Foot I cite as an example." The attack was obviously so devastating that he had never forgotten it.

I was invited not long afterwards to our old college, Univ, to give a talk to the students by the Master, Robin Butler, who had been a contemporary of ours at the college. I suggested to Robin that he ought to invite Paul to speak on his favourite subject of Shelley, who been sent down from the same college in 1811 after publishing his pamphlet on The Necessity of Atheism. Rather surprisingly, Robin took me up on it and, even more surprisingly, Paul accepted – though as a fellow atheist he declined the invitation to accompany the Master to evensong and refused to dress up specially. His son Tom drove him to Oxford; there was a crowded gathering in the Master's Lodge and he was altogether delighted by his reception.

A more memorable occasion was our visit together to the Festival Hall for a Brahms concert, consisting of the 2nd Piano Concerto and the Fourth Symphony – both great favourites since Oxford days. It was quite a performance getting Paul to the South Bank, where he was able to park in the disabled bay and make it to the lift. But the effort was worth it: the playing was wonderful, a reminder of all the music we had listened to over the years. Afterwards he drove me to Paddington, a rather frightening experience, as more than once he seemed keen to drive through a red light.

I suppose both of us were aware that we might not be together for much longer. Even so, the end, when it came, was a terrible shock. He had remained active to the last and had filed copy to Private Eye shortly before he left for Ireland. Yet, from an objective standpoint, it was "a good way to go". The day-to-day business of life had become such a struggle, and behind it lay the fear that he could end up seriously disabled and dependent on others for care.

Apart from his family, his loss was perhaps most keenly felt at the offices of Private Eye, where he had become like part of the furniture. For years we had been familiar with the triumphant cry from his desk, "We've got him! We've got the bastard!". Everyone there, especially the girls, loved him. I had become accustomed to seeing his sticks at the bottom of the staircase, a sign that he was in the building. As a journalist he was irreplaceable. No one could rival the quantity of his output or his ability to turn his mind to any subject.

For myself, I had lost the friend who had accompanied me on my journalistic journey since our time at school and Oxford. I felt, and still feel, his absence like a great hole in my life. He had helped me to work out a route, supported and assisted me even when he was working for other people. From now on I would have to go it alone.

CHRONOLOGY

1937   Born in Haifa, Palestine.

1947-55 Boarder at Ludgrove then Shrewsbury where he meets Christopher Booker, Richard Ingrams and Willie Rushton. All four go on to edit the school magazine, the *Salopian*.

1955-7 National service with the army in Yorkshire then Jamaica.

1958-61 Studies law at University College, Oxford.

1958   Joins CND and goes on the first Aldermaston march for peace.

1959   Paul and Richard Ingrams edit the undergraduate magazine *Parson's Pleasure* while at University College Oxford.

1961   Appointed editor of *Isis*, another of the university's magazines. Joins Glasgow *Daily Record*. The first edition of *Private Eye* is published on 25 October 1961.

1962   Marries Monica Beckinsale.

1964   Returns to London and works for six months on the *Sun*, previously the *Daily Herald*. Starts to make occasional contributions to *Private Eye*.

       Son John born.

1965   Begins a two-year stint with the *Sunday Telegraph*. November – Paul writes in *Private Eye* that "James Hanratty was not guilty." Hanratty was hanged three years previously for the A6 murder.

1966   September – reveals development of germ warfare at Porton Down. The magazine is requested by the Home Office not to print anything more on the matter "in the interests of security".

       Son Matt born.

1967 31 March – joins *Private Eye* full-time.

1968 Arkell v Pressdram – *Private Eye*'s first libel victory, over a Footnotes story about a corrupt security firm in the Midlands.

10 May – first mention of Dr Christiaan Barnard's heart transplants, pointing out that despite widespread positive coverage, the process was largely untested and unable to save patients' lives.

30 August – Paul's first report on the collapse of Ronan Point. He reveals engineers' reports concluding that many similar prefabricated towers are "more likely to fall down than to stay up".

December *Hearts and Grafts*, a special supplement of Paul's pieces on the "heart transplant craze" published.

1969 11 April – Paul reveals that his old housemaster at Shrewsbury, now headmaster of Eton, Anthony Chenevix Trench, was an enthusiastic flogger of boys.

1970 24 April – Paul reveals that Reginald Maudling, now home secretary, also had a number of business connections with the troubled business empire run by architect John Poulson and local politician T. Dan Smith.

1971 2 March – "The Balsoff Memorandum" printed in Footnotes. Nora Beloff of the *Observer* sues for breach of copyright, and loses.

27 July – Paul marries Rose Harvey.

Who Killed Hanratty? published.

1972 August – Reginald Maudling resigns from the cabinet over the Poulson affair.

October – Paul Foot leaves *Private Eye* to work for *Socialist Worker*, which he later edits. Three months later he wins Journalist of the Year award from *What the Papers Say*.
He continues to contribute to the magazine on a freelance basis.

1975	Birmingham Six and Guildford Four imprisoned after bomb attacks. Paul begins to campaign against convictions.
1978	July – Paul reports that Jeremy Thorpe will be arrested in the Norman Scott affair. Thorpe issues a writ. He is arrested two weeks later.
1979	Starts weekly investigative column in *Daily Mirror* which he writes for the next fourteen years, while still contributing to *Private Eye*.
	June – first report in the *Eye* on the suspicious death of Helen Smith, a nurse, in Saudi Arabia.
	June – Jeremy Thorpe goes on trial for conspiracy to murder. He is found not guilty.
	November – Bridgewater Four imprisoned for murder of newspaper boy Carl Bridgewater. Paul begins to campaign against their false conviction the following year.
	Son Tom born.
1982	December – inquest into death of Helen Smith finally held. Jury rejects verdict of accidental death after hearing details of her injuries.
1983	*The Helen Smith Story* published.
1986	*Murder at the Farm:Who Killed Carl Bridgewater?* published.
	June – accuses MI5 of attempts to discredit Deputy Chief Constable John Stalker following his investigations into the RUC's "Shoot to Kill" policy. He is later cleared of misconduct.
	September – raises questions about another possible suspect in Bridgewater Four case.
	Ian Hislop becomes editor of *Private Eye* following Richard Ingrams' retirement.
1987	April – first report on Colin Wallace, who was sacked from MoD after refusing to work on operations aimed at destabilising Harold Wilson's government and subsequently imprisoned for manslaughter.

1988 March – first report on the Gibraltar killings of three unarmed IRA members by the SAS.

1989 January – Paul's first report on Lockerbie, in which he notes that "the view of many – that Palestinian extremists planted the bomb – may not be too far away from the truth".

February – *Rock Bottom*, a special *Private Eye* report on the government and press cover-up of the Gibraltar killings, published.

September – Paul reveals in the *Daily Mirror* that Sonia Sutcliffe was paid £25,000 by the *Mail on Sunday* via an intermediary. This forms an important part of *Private Eye*'s successful appeal against the record £600,000 damages Sutcliffe had been awarded earlier that year.

October – Guildford Four released by court of appeal after 15 years in prison.

Second Journalist of the Year award from *What the Papers Say*.

Who Framed Colin Wallace? published.

Starts living with Clare Fermont.

1990 January – reports on new evidence of innocence of Birmingham Six and predicts their imminent release.

1991 March – Birmingham Six cleared by Court of Appeal and released from prison after 16 years.

November – a special report on Lockerbie by Paul is sceptical about the US Justice Department's announcement that Libyan intelligence agents were responsible.

Writes letter in *Guardian* calling for formation of Media Workers Against the War (the first war in Iraq), and hundreds respond. Edit's MWAW newsletter and chairs mass meetings.

1992 May – In the first of many reports on the business activities of Jonathan Aitken, minister for defence procurement, Paul points out that he had been a director of an arms dealing company on whose behalf he had negotiated with the Saudi royal family.

July – first notes the harassment of relatives of the Cardiff Three, dubiously convicted of the murder of a prostitute four years previously. Their convictions are overturned later that year.

1993   May – Paul Foot leaves *Mirror* after a long NUJ campaign against the new management and devotes his final (unpublished) column to David Montgomery's purge of staff there. Returns to *Private Eye* and Footnotes column and writes a fortnightly column in the *Guardian*.

1994   May – Paul's coverage of the Scott Inquiry into arms to Iraq begins. In November *Private Eye* publishes *Not the Scott Report: Thatcher, Major, Saddam and the Merchants of Death*, a special edition co-authored with Tim Laxton, which wins the George Orwell Prize for Journalism.

The Court of Appeal clears Eddie Browning of the "M50 murder" of Marie Wilks, which Paul has been reporting on for the *Daily Mirror* for a number of years.

December – first report on the Private Finance Initiative, which has led to disasters in the social security department and the Channel tunnel rail link.

Daughter Kate born.

1995   April – the jury in the inquest into the Marchioness disaster return a verdict of unlawful killing.

1996   March – Jonathan Aitken turns his "simple sword of truth and trusty shield of British fair play" against *Private Eye* and sues for libel over the latest of Foot's series of articles about him, which accused him of being a serial liar. The magazine's legal costs are eventually paid by the trustees of Aitken's estate after he is declared bankrupt and jailed for perjury.

April – reports that social worker Alison Taylor was first ignored, then sacked and smeared by police for making (accurate) allegations of child abuse in North Wales.

July – Colin Wallace cleared of manslaughter fifteen years after his conviction.

1997   February – Bridgewater Four finally cleared and released after 18 years in prison.

1998   April – Paul picks holes in the prosecution case against two Palestinians jailed for bombing the Israeli Embassy in London, and reports on rogue MI5 agent David Shayler's claims that warnings about an imminent terrorist attack were ignored.

July – reveals that senior MI5 officials believed the bombing of the Israeli Embassy to have been carried out by the Israelis themselves to force Britain to provide better security.

1999   January – first story about Sergeant Gurpal Virdi, who was arrested and accused of sending racist hate mail after complaining about racism in Metropolitan police. He is later sacked.

February – Paul points out that the Private Finance Initiative, now enthusiastically adopted by Labour, is creating new hospitals that are more expensive, with fewer nurses and beds than before.

April   Paul's last piece on James Hanratty pointing out that new DNA evidence which linked him to the murders 38 years before may well have been contaminated and unreliable. His murder conviction is later upheld by the Court of Appeal.

April – Paul suffers a thoracic aortic aneurysm.

August – Department of Transport announces judicial inquiry into Marchioness disaster.

November – Paul returns to work at *Private Eye*.

2000   February – the Waterhouse Inquiry into child abuse in North Wales concludes that Alison Taylor's allegations fourteen years earlier were vindicated.

March – receives special *What The Papers Say* Award as campaigning journalist of the decade.

July – the three convicted men in the M25 murder case are released by the Court of Appeal.

2001   May – special edition *Lockerbie: The Flight From Justice* published following the conviction of a Libyan intelligence agent for murder.

November – Court of Appeal dismisses appeals of two accused of Israeli Embassy bombing after the government applies for Public Interest Immunity certificates to ensure that David Shayler's evidence cannot be considered.

2002   February – reveals that 600 buildings belonging to Inland Revenue and Customs have been sold to Mapeley Ltd, a company based in a tax haven.

February – Sergeant Gurpal Virdi returns to police force with £240,000 compensation after an employment tribunal rules he was victim of racial discrimination.

September – reports that fourteen years after the Piper Alpha disaster, BP is planning to abandon stand-by ships in favour of helicopters, against the recommendations of the Cullen report into the tragedy.

2003   May – *The Artful Dodgers*, a special report on the Inland Revenue/Mapeley deal and the government's attempts to cover it up, published.

November – Paul's last piece in *Eye* on death of Helen Smith.

2004   March – *P.F. Eye: An Idiot's Guide to the Private Finance Initiative* detailing "how it became a jewel in the crown of New Labour, its savings, its costs, its pitfalls and windfalls, and how it changed the face of British accountancy and British politics" published.

July – Paul Foot dies of a heart attack.

BIBLIOGRAPHY

Books

Immigration and Race in British Politics (1965)

The Politics of Harold Wilson (1968)

The Rise of Enoch Powell (1969)

Who Killed Hanratty? (1971)

Why You Should be a Socialist (1977)

Red Shelley (1981)

The Helen Smith Story (1983)

Murder on the Farm, Who Killed Carl Bridgewater? (1986)

Who Framed Colin Wallace? (1989)

Words as Weapons (1990)

Articles of Resistance (2000).

The Vote: How it was won, and how it was undermined (2005)

Private Eye Specials

Hearts and Grafts – An Examination of the Heart Transplant Craze (Issue 183, 1968)

Rock Bottom – The Gibraltar Killings – Government and Press Cover-Up (February 1989)

Ripping Yarns – Sonia Sutcliffe – The Press and The Law (March 1991)

Not the Scott Report – Arms to Iraq Special (November 1994)

Lockerbie – The Flight from Justice May/June 2001

Tax Dodge Report – The Artful Dodgers – Inland Revenue/Mapeley deal (Issue 1080, 2003)

P.F. Eye – An Idiot's guide to the Private Finance Initiative (Issue 1102, 2004)

PICTURE CREDITS:
Jane Bown – Inside back cover
flap
Guardian Newspapers Ltd 2004
– p5
Lord Gowrie – p11
Eric Hands – p64